Exploring Splunk

SEARCH PROCESSING LANGUAGE (SPL)
PRIMER AND COOKBOOK

By David Carasso, Splunk's Chief Mind

CITO
Research
New York, NY

Exploring Splunk, by David Carasso

Published by CITO Research, 1375 Broadway, Fl3, New York, NY 10018.

Editor/Analyst: Dan Woods, Deb Cameron

Copyeditor: Deb Cameron

Production Editor: Deb Gabriel

Cover: Splunk, Inc.

Graphics: Deb Gabriel

First Edition: April 2012

While every precaution has been taken in the preparation of this book, the publisher and author assume no responsibility for errors or omissions or for damages resulting from the use of the information contained herein.

ISBN: 978-0-9825506-7-0; 0-9825506-7-7

Disclaimer

This book is intended as a text and reference book for reading purposes only. The actual use of Splunk's software products must be in accordance with their corresponding software license agreements and not with anything written in this book. The documentation provided for Splunk's software products, and not this book, is the definitive source for information on how to use these products.

Although great care has been taken to ensure the accuracy and timeliness of the information in this book, Splunk does not give any warranty or guarantee of the accuracy or timeliness of the information and Splunk does not assume any liability in connection with any use or result from the use of the information in this book. The reader should check at docs.splunk.com for definitive descriptions of Splunk's features and functionality.

Table of Contents

Preface

About This Book   i

What's In This Book?   ii

Conventions   ii

Acknowledgments   iii

PART I: EXPLORING SPLUNK

1   The Story of Splunk

Splunk to the Rescue in the Datacenter   3

Splunk to the Rescue in the Marketing Department   4

Approaching Splunk   5

Splunk: The Company and the Concept   7

How Splunk Mastered Machine Data in the Datacenter   8

Operational Intelligence   9

Operational Intelligence at Work   11

2   Getting Data In

Machine Data Basics   13

     Types of Data Splunk Can Read   15

     Splunk Data Sources   15

     Downloading, Installing, and Starting Splunk   15

Bringing Data in for Indexing   17

Understanding How Splunk Indexes Data   18

3   Searching with Splunk

The Search Dashboard   23

SPL™: Search Processing Language   27

Pipes 27

Implied AND 28

top user 28

fields – percent 28

The search Command 29

Tips for Using the search Command 30

Subsearches 30

4 SPL: Search Processing Language

Sorting Results 33

sort 33

Filtering Results 35

where 35

dedup 36

head 38

Grouping Results 39

transaction 39

Reporting Results 41

top 41

stats 43

chart 45

timechart 47

Filtering, Modifying, and Adding Fields 48

fields 49

replace 50

eval 51

rex 52

lookup 53

5 Enriching Your Data

Using Splunk to Understand Data 55

Identifying Fields: Looking at the Pieces of the Puzzle 56

Exploring the Data to Understand its Scope   58

Preparing for Reporting and Aggregation   60

Visualizing Data   65

Creating Visualizations   65

Creating Dashboards   67

Creating Alerts   68

Creating Alerts through a Wizard   68

Tuning Alerts Using Manager   71

Customizing Actions for Alerting   74

The Alerts Manager   74

PART II: RECIPES

6   **Recipes for Monitoring and Alerting**

Monitoring Recipes   79

Monitoring Concurrent Users   79

Monitoring Inactive Hosts   80

Reporting on Categorized Data   81

Comparing Today's Top Values to Last Month's   82

Finding Metrics That Fell by 10% in an Hour   84

Charting Week Over Week Results   85

Identify Spikes in Your Data   86

Compacting Time-Based Charting   88

Reporting on Fields Inside XML or JSON   88

Extracting Fields from an Event   89

Alerting Recipes   90

Alerting by Email when a Server Hits a Predefined Load   90

Alerting When Web Server Performance Slows   91

Shutting Down Unneeded EC2 Instances   91

Converting Monitoring to Alerting   92

7 Grouping Events

Introduction	95
Recipes	97
Unifying Field Names	97
Finding Incomplete Transactions	97
Calculating Times within Transactions	99
Finding the Latest Events	100
Finding Repeated Events	101
Time Between Transactions	102
Finding Specific Transactions	104
Finding Events Near Other Events	107
Finding Events After Events	108
Grouping Groups	109

8 Lookup Tables

Introduction	113
lookup	113
inputlookup	113
outputlookup	113
Further Reading	114
Recipes	114
Setting Default Lookup Values	114
Using Reverse Lookups	114
Using a Two-Tiered Lookup	116
Using Multistep Lookups	116
Creating a Lookup Table from Search Results	117
Appending Results to Lookup Tables	117
Using Massive Lookup Tables	118
Comparing Results to Lookup Values	120

Controlling Lookup Matches................................122
Matching IPs................................122
Matching with Wildcards................................123

Appendix A: Machine Data Basics

Application Logs................................126
Web Access Logs................................126
Web Proxy Logs................................127
Call Detail Records................................127
Clickstream Data................................127
Message Queuing................................128
Packet Data................................128
Configuration Files................................128
Database Audit Logs and Tables................................128
File System Audit Logs................................128
Management and Logging APIs................................129
OS Metrics, Status, and Diagnostic Commands................................129
Other Machine Data Sources................................129

Appendix B: Case Sensitivity

Appendix C: Top Commands

Appendix D: Top Resources

Appendix E: Splunk Quick Reference Guide

CONCEPTS................................137
Overview................................137
Events................................137
Sources and Sourcetypes................................138
Hosts................................138
Indexes................................138
Fields................................138
Tags................................138

Event Types   139

Reports and Dashboards   139

Apps   139

Permissions/Users/Roles   139

Transactions   139

Forwarder/Indexer   140

SPL   140

Subsearches   141

Relative Time Modifiers   141

COMMON SEARCH COMMANDS   142

Optimizing Searches   142

SEARCH EXAMPLES   143

EVAL FUNCTIONS   146

COMMON STATS FUNCTIONS   151

REGULAR EXPRESSIONS   152

COMMON SPLUNK STRPTIME FUNCTIONS   153

Preface

Splunk Enterprise Software ("Splunk") is probably the single most powerful tool for searching and exploring data that you will ever encounter. We wrote this book to provide an introduction to Splunk and all it can do. This book also serves as a jumping off point for how to get creative with Splunk.

Splunk is often used by system administrators, network administrators, and security gurus, but its use is not restricted to these audiences. There is a great deal of business value hidden away in corporate data that Splunk can liberate. This book is designed to reach beyond the typical techie reader of O'Reilly books to marketing quants as well as everyone interested in the topics of Big Data and Operational Intelligence.

About This Book

The central goal of this book is to help you rapidly understand what Splunk is and how it can help you. It accomplishes this by teaching you the most important parts of Splunk's Search Processing Language (SPL™). Splunk can help technologists and businesspeople in many ways. Don't expect to learn Splunk all at once. Splunk is more like a Swiss army knife, a simple tool that can do many powerful things.

Now the question becomes: How can this book help? The short answer is by quickly giving you a sense of what you can do with Splunk and pointers on where to learn more.

But isn't there already a lot of Splunk documentation? Yes:

- If you check out http://docs.splunk.com, you will find many manuals with detailed explanations of the machinery of Splunk.

- If you check out http://splunkbase.com, you will find a searchable database of questions and answers. This sort of content is invaluable when you know a bit about Splunk and are trying to solve common problems.

This book falls in between these two levels of documentation. It offers a basic understanding of Splunk's most important parts and combines it with solutions to real-world problems.

What's In This Book?

Chapter 1 tells you what Splunk is and how it can help you.

Chapter 2 discusses how to download Splunk and get started.

Chapter 3 discusses the search user interface and searching with Splunk.

Chapter 4 covers the most commonly used parts of the SPL.

Chapter 5 explains how to visualize and enrich your data with knowledge.

Chapter 6 covers the most common monitoring and alerting solutions.

Chapter 7 covers solutions to problems that can be solved by grouping events.

Chapter 8 covers many of the ways you can use lookup tables to solve common problems.

If you think of Part I (chapters 1 through 5) as a crash course in Splunk, Part II (chapters 6 through 8) shows you how to do some advanced maneuvers by putting it all together, using Splunk to solve some common and interesting problems. By reviewing these recipes—and trying a few—you'll get ideas about how you can use Splunk to help you answer all the mysteries of the universe (or at least of the data center).

The appendices round out the book with some helpful information. Appendix A provides an overview of the basics of machine data to open your eyes to the possibilities and variety of Big Data. Appendix B provides a table on what is and isn't case-sensitive in Splunk searches. Appendix C provides a glimpse into the most common searches run with Splunk (we figured this out using Splunk, by the way). Appendix D offers pointers to some of the best resources for learning more about Splunk. Appendix E is a specially designed version of the Splunk Reference card, which is the most popular educational document we have.

Conventions

As you read through this book, you'll notice we use various fonts to call out certain elements:

- UI elements appear in **bold**.
- Commands and field names are in `constant width`.

If you are told to select the **Y** option from the **X** menu, that's written concisely as "select **X** » **Y**."

Acknowledgments

This book would not have been possible without the help of numerous people at Splunk who gave of their time and talent. For carefully reviewing drafts of the manuscript and making invaluable improvements, we'd like to thank Ledion Bitincka, Gene Hartsell, Gerald Kanapathy, Vishal Patel, Alex Raitz, Stephen Sorkin, Sophy Ting, and Steve Zhang, PhD; for generously giving interview time: Maverick Garner; for additional help: Jessica Law, Tera Mendonca, Rachel Perkins, and Michael Wilde.

PART I
EXPLORING SPLUNK

1 The Story of Splunk

Splunk is a powerful platform for analyzing machine data, data that machines emit in great volumes but which is seldom used effectively. Machine data is already important in the world of technology and is becoming increasingly important in the world of business. (To learn more about machine data, see Appendix A.)

The fastest way to understand the power and versatility of Splunk is to consider two scenarios: one in the datacenter and one in the marketing department.

Splunk to the Rescue in the Datacenter

It's 2 AM on Wednesday. The phone rings. Your boss is calling; the website is down. Why did it fail? Was it the web servers, the applications, the database servers, a full disk, or load balancers on the fritz? He's yelling at you to fix it now. It's raining. You're freaking out.

Relax. You deployed Splunk yesterday.

You start up Splunk. From one place, you can search the log files from all your web servers, databases, firewalls, routers, and load balancers, as well as search configuration files and data from all your other devices, operating systems, or applications of interest. (This is true no matter how many datacenters or cloud providers these may be scattered across.)

You look at a graph of web server traffic to see when the problem happened. At 5:03 PM, errors on the web servers spiked dramatically. You then look at the top 10 pages with errors. The home page is okay. The search page is okay. Ah, the shopping cart is the problem. Starting at 5:03, every request to that page produced an error. This is costing money—preventing sales and driving away customers—and it must be fixed.

You know that your shopping cart relies on an ecommerce server connected to a database. A look at the logs shows the database is up. Good. Let's look at the ecommerce server logs. At 5:03 PM, the ecommerce server starts saying it cannot connect to the database server. You then search for changes to the configuration files and see that someone changed a network setting. You look closer; it was done incorrectly. You contact the person who made the change, who rolls it back, and the system starts working again.

All of this can take less than 5 minutes because Splunk gathered all of the relevant information into a central index that you could rapidly search.

Splunk to the Rescue in the Marketing Department

You work in the promotions department of a large retailer. You tune the search engine optimization and promotions for your products to optimize the yield of incoming traffic. Last week, the guys from the datacenter installed a new Splunk dashboard that shows (for the past hour, day, and week) all the search terms used to find your site.

Looking at the graph for the last few hours, you see a spike 20 minutes ago. Searches for your company name and your latest product are way up. You check a report on top referring URLs in the past hour and Splunk shows that a celebrity tweeted about the product and linked to your home page.

You look at another graph that shows performance of the most frequently visited pages. The search page is overloaded and slowing down. A huge crowd of people is coming to your site but can't find the product they are looking for, so they are all using search.

You log on to your site's content management system and put a promotional ad for the new product at the center of the home page. You then go back and look at the top pages. Search traffic starts to drop, and traffic to the new product page starts to rise, and so does traffic to the shopping cart page. You look at the top 10 products added to the cart and the top 10 products purchased; the new product tops the list. You send a note to the PR department to follow up. Incoming traffic is now converting to sales instead of frustration, exactly what you want to happen. Your ability to make the most of an unforeseen opportunity was made possible by Splunk. Your next step is to make sure that you have enough of that product in stock, a great problem to have.

These two examples show how Splunk can provide a detailed window into what is happening in your machine data. Splunk can also reveal historical trends, correlate multiple sources of information, and help in thousands of other ways.

Approaching Splunk

As you use Splunk to answer questions, you'll find that you can break the task into three phases.

- First, identify the data that can answer your question.

- Second, transform the data into the results that can answer your question.

- Third, display the answer in a report, interactive chart, or graph to make it intelligible to a wide range of audiences.

Begin with the questions you want to answer: Why did that system fail? Why is it so slow lately? Where are people having trouble with our website? As you master Splunk, it becomes more obvious what types of data and searches help answer those questions. This book will accelerate your progress to mastery.

The question then becomes: Can the data provide the answers? Often, when we begin an analysis, we don't know what the data can tell us. But Splunk is also a powerful tool for exploring data and getting to know it. You can discover the most common values or the most unusual. You can summarize the data with statistics or group events into transactions, such as all the events that make up an online hotel reservation across systems of record. You can create workflows that begin with the whole data set, then filter out irrelevant events, analyzing what's left. Then, perhaps, add some information from an external source until, after a number of simple steps, you have only the data needed to answer your questions. Figure 1-1 shows, in general, the basic Splunk analysis processes.

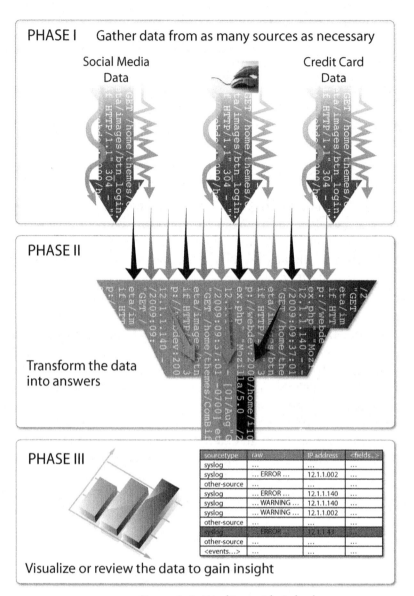

Figure 1-1. Working with Splunk

Splunk: The Company and the Concept

The real excitement most people feel about Splunk comes from its ability to help solve the complex and recurring problems that Splunk customers have always had. The story of Splunk began in 2002, when cofounders Erik Swan and Rob Das started looking around for their next challenge. Erik and Rob had done a couple of startups together and were looking for an idea for a new venture, so they started talking to companies about their problems.

Erik and Rob asked prospective customers, "How do you solve problems in your infrastructure?" Over and over again, Erik and Rob heard about practitioner's experiences trying to troubleshoot IT problems and retrieve data by traditional means. The data was too spread out; it was hard to bring it all together and make sense of it. Everyone was attempting to solve problems by manually poring over log files, sometimes writing scripts to help them along. The homegrown scripts were brittle, the people who wrote them sometimes left the company and took their expertise with them, and every new attempt to explore an issue would result in finger-pointing, buck-passing, and script rebuilding, with heavy-duty custom assistance from the IT department. These practitioners told Splunk's founders that solving infrastructure problems was like slowly crawling around in caves (their datacenters) with pickaxes, poor lighting, and limited navigational power (old scripts and log management technologies). In short, it was like spelunking—and so, the name "Splunk" was born.

Given the difficulty of digital spelunking, the only alternative available to these people was to search the Web to see if other companies had similar problems and had posted solutions online. The founders were stunned that people were spending money on this widely acknowledged issue, and yet no one had stepped up to solve the problem. Erik and Rob asked themselves, "Why couldn't searching IT data be as easy and intuitive as a Google™ search?"

The first vision of Splunk was aimed at making it much easier to assemble and analyze the data needed to run and troubleshoot a datacenter or large computing or networking environment. The mission of Splunk was to combine the ease of a web search with the power of the laborious, homegrown methods IT professionals were using to troubleshoot problems.

Erik and Rob raised funding and the first version of Splunk debuted at LinuxWorld® 2005. The product was a huge hit and immediately went viral, spurred on by its availability as a free download. Once downloaded, Splunk began solving broad range of unimagined customer problems and spread from department to department and from company to company. When users asked management to purchase it, they could already point to a record of solving problems and saving time with Splunk.

Originally conceived to help IT and datacenter managers troubleshoot technical problems, Splunk has grown to become an extremely useful platform for all kinds of business users because it enables them to search, collect, and organize data in a far more comprehensive, far less labor-intensive way than traditional databases. The result is new business insights and operational intelligence that organizations have never had before.

How Splunk Mastered Machine Data in the Datacenter

The first place that Splunk took hold, naturally, was the datacenter, which is awash in machine data. Splunk became popular with system administrators, network engineers, and application developers as an engine to quickly understand (and increase the usefulness of) machine data. But why did they like it so much? An example helps not only explain Splunk's early popularity but also helps us understand the nature of machine data, which is central to the larger value that Splunk brings to the business world.

In most computing environments, many different systems depend on each other. Monitoring systems send alerts after something goes wrong. For example, the key web pages of a site may depend on web servers, application servers, database servers, file systems, load balancers, routers, application accelerators, caching systems, and so on. When something goes wrong in one of these systems, say a database, alarms may start sounding at all levels, seemingly at once. When this happens, a system administrator or application specialist must find the root cause and fix it. The problem is that the log files are spread across multiple machines, sometimes in different time zones, and contain millions of entries, most of which have nothing to do with the problem. In addition, the relevant records—the ones that indicate some failure of the system—tend to appear all at once. The challenge then is to find the problem that started it all. Let's look at how Splunk helps do this.

- Splunk begins with indexing, which means gathering all the data from diverse locations and combining it into centralized indexes. Before Splunk, system administrators would have had to log in to many different machines to gain access to all the data using far less powerful tools.

- Using the indexes, Splunk can quickly search the logs from all servers and hone in on when the problem occurred. With its speed, scale, and usability, Splunk makes determining when a problem occurred that much faster.

- Splunk can then drill down into the time period when the problem first occurred to determine its root cause. Alerts can then be created to head the issue off in the future.

By indexing and aggregating log files from many sources to make them centrally searchable, Splunk has become popular among system administrators and other people who run technical operations for businesses around the world. Security analysts use Splunk to sniff out security vulnerabilities and attacks. System analysts use Splunk to discover inefficiencies and bottlenecks in complex applications. Network analysts use Splunk to find the cause of network outages and bandwidth bottlenecks.

This discussion brings up several key points about Splunk:

- **Creating a central repository is vital:** One of the major victories of Splunk is the way that diverse types of data from many different sources are centralized for searching.

- **Splunk converts data into answers:** Splunk helps you find the insights that are buried in the data.

- **Splunk helps you understand the structure and meaning of data:** The more you understand your data, the more you'll see in it. Splunk also helps you capture what you learn to make future investigations easier and to share what you've learned with others.

- **Visualization closes the loop:** All that indexing and searching pays off when you see a chart or a report that makes an answer crystal clear. Being able to visualize data in different ways accelerates understanding and helps you share that understanding with others.

Operational Intelligence

Because almost everything we do is assisted in some way by technology, the information collected about each of us has grown dramatically. Many of the events recorded by servers actually represent behavior of customers or partners. Splunk customers figured out early on that web server access logs could be used not only to diagnose systems but also to better understand the behavior of the people browsing a website.

Splunk has been at the forefront of raising awareness about operational intelligence, a new category of methods and technology for using machine data to gain visibility into the business and discover insights for IT and the entire enterprise. Operational intelligence is not an outgrowth of business intelligence (BI), but a new approach based on sources of information not typically within the purview of BI solutions. Operational data is not only incredibly valuable for improving IT operations, but also for yielding insights into other parts of the business.

Operational intelligence enables organizations to:

- **Use machine data to gain a deeper understanding of their customers:** For example, if you just track transactions on a website, you see what people bought. But by looking closely at the web server logs you can see all the pages they looked at before they purchased, and, perhaps even more important for the bottom line, you can see the pages that the people who didn't buy looked at. (Remember our new product search example from the intro?)

- **Reveal important patterns and analytics derived from correlating events from many sources:** When you can track indicators of consumer behavior from websites, call detail records, social media, and in-store retail transactions, a far more complete picture of the customer emerges. As more and more customer interactions show up in machine data, more can be learned.

- **Reduce the time between an important event and its detection:** Machine data can be monitored and correlated in real time.

- **Leverage live feeds and historical data to make sense of what is happening now, to find trends and anomalies, and to make more informed decisions based on that information:** For example, the traffic created by a web promotion can be measured in real time and compared with previous promotions.

- **Deploy a solution quickly and deliver the flexibility needed by organizations today and in the future—that is, the ability to provide ad hoc reports, answer questions, and add new data sources:** Splunk data can be presented in traditional dashboards that allow users to explore the events and keep asking new questions.

Operational Intelligence at Work

Splunk does something that no other product can: efficiently capture and analyze massive amounts of unstructured, time-series textual machine data. Although IT departments generally start out using Splunk to solve technically esoteric problems, they quickly gain insights valuable elsewhere in their business.

Using machine data in Splunk helps solve vexing business problems. Here are a few examples:

- An operations team implemented a cloud-delivered customer-facing application and used Splunk for diagnostics. They soon realized they could track user statistics and better plan capacity—a metric with profound business implications.

- Web server traffic logs can be used to track shopping carts being filled and abandoned in real time. The marketing department can use this information to determine where consumers are getting stuck and what types of purchases are being abandoned so that any problems can be fixed right away and promotions can target items that are abandoned.

- Organizations using Splunk to monitor applications for troubleshooting have realized that they can easily provide views to their first-line support team to handle customer calls directly, versus escalating those calls to expensive engineering resources.

- A major utility company was able to eliminate costly software maintenance fees by replacing six other monitoring and diagnostic tools with Splunk, while enhancing their NERC and SOX compliance efforts.

- A major public media organization reduced the time it took to capture critical web analytics from months to hours. They were also able to track their digital assets with a granularity and accuracy that they couldn't have otherwise, resulting in better royalty accounting and content marketing.

- A taco fast-food restaurant connected its points of sale (POS) to Splunk, and within an hour, business analysts were able to begin answering questions like, "How many people are buying tacos in the midnight-to-2 AM period, in this geography, during this time of the year?"

Ultimately, operational intelligence enables organizations to ask the right questions, leading to answers that deliver business insights, using combinations of real-time and historical data, displayed in easily digestible dashboards and graphical tools.

There's a reason for the trend toward calling machine data "big data." It's big, it's messy, and in there, buried somewhere, is the key to the future of your business. Now let's move on to Chapter 2, where you'll learn how to get data into Splunk and start finding the gold hidden in your data.

2 Getting Data In

Chapter 1 provided an introduction to Splunk and described how it can help you. Now let's take the next step in your journey: getting your data into Splunk.

This chapter covers installing Splunk, importing your data, and a bit about how the data is organized to facilitate searching.

Machine Data Basics

Splunk's mission is to make machine data useful for people. To give you some context, it's worth reviewing a few basics about machine data and how Splunk keeps track of it.

People who create systems (such as web servers or load balancers or video games or social media platforms) also specify the information those systems write to log files when they are running. This information (the machine data in the log files) is what people using the systems can use to understand what those systems are doing as they run (or fail to run). For example, the log file output for a hypothetical clock application might look like this:

```
Action: ticked s:57, m:05, h:10, d:23, mo:03, y:2011
Action: ticked s:58, m:05, h:10, d:23, mo:03, y:2011
Action: ticked s:59, m:05, h:10, d:23, mo:03, y:2011
Action: ticked s:00, m:06, h:10, d:23, mo:03, y:2011
```

Every time the clock ticks, it logs the action and the time that the action occurred. If you were really going to keep track of the clock, in addition to the fact that it ticked, the log might also include other useful information: the battery level, when an alarm was set, turned on or off, or sounded—anything that could give you insight into how the clock was working. Each line of the machine data shown above can be considered a separate event, although it's common for other machine data to have events that span multiple or even hundreds of lines.

Splunk divides raw machine data into discrete pieces of information known as *events*. When you do a simple search, Splunk retrieves the events that match your search terms. Each event consists of discrete pieces of data known as fields. In clock data, the fields might include second, minute, hour, day, month, and year. If you think of groups of events organized in a spreadsheet or database, the events are the rows and the fields are the columns, as shown in Figure 2-1.

Second	Minute	Hour	Day	Month	Year
58	1	14	23	11	2011
59	1	14	23	11	2011
60	1	14	23	11	2011
1	2	14	23	11	2011
2	2	14	23	11	2011
3	2	14	23	11	2011

Figure 2-1. Clock Events in a Spreadsheet Form

In practice, another way to think of events is as a set of fields of keyword/value pairs. If represented as keyword/value pairs, the clock events look like Figure 2-2.

```
Second=58, Minute=01, Hour=14, Day=23, Year=2011
Second=59, Minute=01, Hour=14, Day=23, Year=2011
Second=60, Minute=01, Hour=14, Day=23, Year=2011
Second=01, Minute=02, Hour=14, Day=23, Year=2011
Second=02, Minute=02, Hour=14, Day=23, Year=2011
```

Figure 2-2. Clock Events as Fields of Keyword/Value Pairs

Here's a real-world example of one of the most common and useful types of machine data. A web server has a log file that records every URL requested from the server.

Some of the fields in web server data are:

```
client IP, timestamp, http method, status, bytes, referrer,
user agent
```

A visit to one webpage can invoke dozens of requests to retrieve text, images, and other resources. Each request is typically logged as a separate event in a log file. The result is a file that looks something like Figure 2-3 (without the fancy highlighting to help you see the fields).

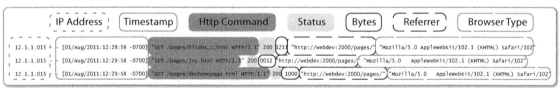

Figure 2-3. Typical Web Server Log

Types of Data Splunk Can Read

One of the common characteristics of machine data is that it almost always contains some indication of when the data was created or when an event described by the data occurred. Given this characteristic, Splunk's indexes are optimized to retrieve events in time-series order. If the raw data does not have an explicit timestamp, Splunk assigns the time at which the event was indexed by Splunk to the events in the data or uses other approximations, such as the time the file was last modified or the timestamp of previous events.

The only other requirement is that the machine data be textual, not binary, data. Image and sound files are common examples of binary data files. Some types of binary files, like the core dump produced when a program crashes, can be converted to textual information, such as a stack trace. Splunk can call your scripts to do that conversion before indexing the data. Ultimately, though, Splunk data must have a textual representation to be indexed and searched.

Splunk Data Sources

During indexing, Splunk can read machine data from any number of sources. The most common input sources are:

- **files:** Splunk can monitor specific files or directories. If data is added to a file or a new file is added to a monitored directory, Splunk reads that data.

- **the network:** Splunk can listen on TCP or UDP ports, reading any data sent.

- **scripted inputs:** Splunk can read the machine data output by programs or scripts, such as a Unix® command or a custom script that monitors sensors.

Enough background: now let's get started working with Splunk.

Downloading, Installing, and Starting Splunk

We recommend that you install Splunk and add some machine data to help you work through the topics discussed in this book. Everything we'll cover can be done using Splunk Free (see below).

This section describes how to get Splunk up and running.

Downloading Splunk

You can download fully functional Splunk for free, for learning or to support small to moderate use of Splunk. On the splunk.com home page, you see this button:

Free Download

Click it to begin downloading and installing Splunk on computers running Windows®, Mac™, Linux®, and Unix.

Installing Splunk

Installing Splunk is easy, so we'll assume you'll do that part on your own. If you have any questions, refer to the Splunk Tutorial (http://splunk.com/goto/book#tutorial), which covers everything in detail.

Starting Splunk

To start Splunk on Windows, launch the application from the Start menu. Look for the Welcome screen, shown in Figure 2-4, and keep reading.

To start Splunk on Mac OS X or Unix, open a terminal window. Go to the directory where you installed Splunk, go to the bin subdirectory and, at the command prompt, type:

```
./splunk start
```

The very last line of the information you see when Splunk starts is:

```
The Splunk web interface is at http://your-machine-
name:8000
```

Follow that link to the login screen. If you don't have a username and password, the default credentials are admin and changeme. After you log in, the Welcome screen appears.

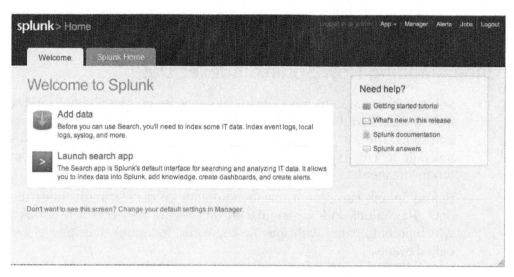

Figure 2-4. The Welcome Screen

The Welcome screen shows what you can do with your pristine instance of Splunk: add data or launch the search app.

Bringing Data in for Indexing

The next step in learning and exploring Splunk is to add some data to the index so you can explore it.

We're going to use some sample data for the purposes of this chapter. You can find instructions for getting this data here: http://splunk.com/goto/book#add_data

There are two steps to the indexing process:

- Downloading the sample file from the Splunk website
- Telling Splunk to index that file

To download the sample file, follow this link and save the file to your desktop: http://splunk.com/goto/book#sample_data

To add the file to Splunk:

1. From the Welcome screen, click **Add Data**.
2. Click **From files and directories** on the bottom half of the screen.
3. Select **Skip preview**.
4. Click the radio button next to **Upload and index a file**.
5. Select the file you downloaded to your desktop.
6. Click **Save**.

You're finished adding your data. Let's talk about what Splunk is doing behind the scenes.

Understanding How Splunk Indexes Data

Splunk's core value to most organizations is its unique ability to index machine data so that it can be quickly searched for analysis, reporting, and alerts. The data that you start with is called raw data. Splunk indexes raw data by creating a time-based map of the words in the data without modifying the data itself.

Before Splunk can search massive amounts of data, it must index the data. The Splunk index is similar to indexes in the back of textbooks, which point to pages with specific keywords. In Splunk, the "pages" are called events.

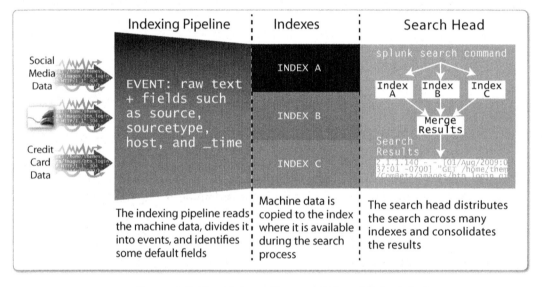

Figure 2-5. The Unique Characteristics of Splunk Indexes

Splunk divides a stream of machine data into individual events. Remember, an event in machine data can be as simple as one line in a log file or as complicated as a stack trace containing several hundred lines.

Every event in Splunk has at least the four default fields shown in Table 2-1.

Table 2-1. Fields Splunk Always Indexes

Field	Answers the question	Examples
source	Where did the data come from?	files (`/var/log/`), scripts (`myscript.bat`), network feeds (`UDP:514`)
sourcetype	What kind of data is it?	`access_combined`, `syslog`
host	Which host or machine did the data come from?	`webserver01`, `cisco_router`
_time	When did the event happen?	`Sat Mar 31 02:16:57 2012`

These default fields are indexed along with the raw data.

The timestamp (`_time`) field is special because Splunk indexers uses it to order events, enabling Splunk to efficiently retrieve events within a time range.

Chapter 3 brings us to the place where most of the action happens: Splunk's search interface.

3 Searching with Splunk

Now that you've gained an understanding of the way Splunk indexes data (in Chapter 2), it will be easier to understand what is happening when you search with Splunk.

Of course, the goal of search is to help you find exactly what you need. It can mean filtering, summarizing, and visualizing a large amount of data, to answer your questions about the data. At other times, you might need to regularly explore large amounts of data. Often, you simply want to find the needle in the haystack, the one buried event that threw everything off.

The **Summary dashboard** gives you a quick overview of the data visible to you. Click **Launch search app** on the Splunk **Welcome** tab. If you're on the Splunk **Home** tab, click **Search** under **Your Apps**. The **Summary dashboard** displays, as shown in Figure 3-1

Figure 3-1. The Search app's Summary dashboard

Notice a few things about this dashboard:

- The **search bar** at the top is empty, ready for you to type in a search.

- The **time range picker** to the right of the **search bar** permits time range adjustment. You can see events from the last 15 minutes, for example, or any desired time interval. For real-time streaming data, you can select an interval to view, ranging from 30 seconds to an hour.

- The **All indexed data** panel displays a running total of the indexed data.

The next three panels show the most recent or common values that have been indexed in each category:

- The **Sources** panel shows which files (or other sources) your data came from.
- The **Source types** panel shows the types of sources in your data.
- The **Hosts** panel shows which hosts your data came from.

Now, let's look at the Search navigation menus near the top of the page:

Figure 3-2. Search navigation menus

- **Summary** is where we are.
- **Search** leads to the main search interface, the **Search dashboard**.
- **Status** lists dashboards on the status of your Splunk instance.
- **Dashboards & Views** lists your dashboards and views.
- **Searches & Reports** lists your saved searches and reports.

The next section introduces you to the **Search dashboard**.

The Search Dashboard

If you click the *Search* option or enter a search in the **search bar**, the page switches to the **Search dashboard** (sometimes called the timeline or flashtimeline view). When a search is kicked off, the results almost immediately start displaying. For example, entering an asterisk (*) in the **search bar** retrieves all the data in your default indexes, and a screen similar to Figure 3-3 appears.

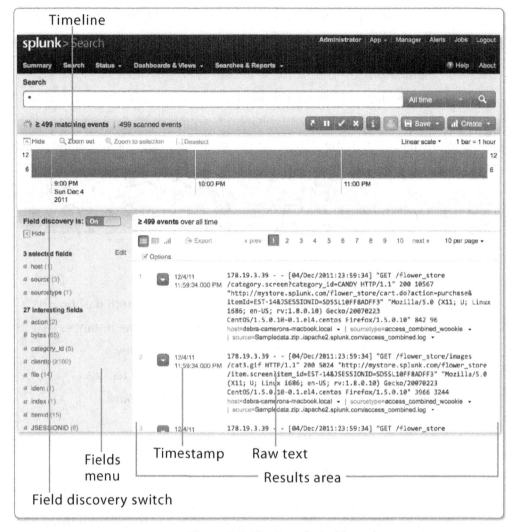

Figure 3-3. The Search dashboard

Let's examine the contents of this dashboard:

- **Timeline:** A graphic representation of the number of events matching your search over time.

- **Fields sidebar:** Relevant fields along with event counts. This menu also allows you to add a field to the results.

- **Field discovery switch:** Turns automatic field discovery on or off. When Splunk executes a search and field discovery is on, Splunk attempts to identify fields automatically for the current search.

- **Results area:** Shows the events from your search. Events are ordered by **Timestamp**, which appears to the left of each event. Beneath the **Raw text** of each event are any fields selected from the **Fields** sidebar for which the event has a value.

When you start typing in the **search bar**, context-sensitive information appears below, with matching searches on the left and help on the right:

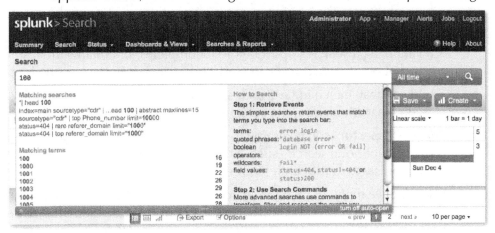

Figure 3-4. Helpful info appears when you enter text in the search bar

Under the **time range picker**, you see a row of icons:

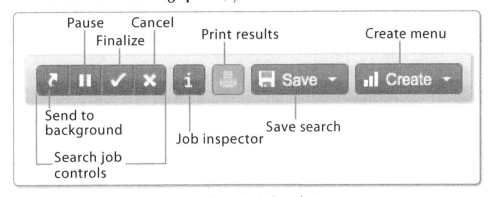

Figure 3-5. Search icons

The **search job controls** are only active when a search is running. If you haven't run a search, or if your search has finished, they are inactive and greyed out. But if you're running a search that takes a long time to complete, you can use these icons to control the search progress:

- Sending a search to the background lets it keep running to completion on the server while you run other searches or even close the window and log out. When you click **Send to background**, the **search bar** clears and you can continue with other tasks. When the job is done, a notification appears on your screen if you're still logged in; otherwise, Splunk emails you (if you've specified an email address). If you want to check on the job in the meantime, or at a later time, click the **Jobs** link at the top of the page.

- Pausing a search temporarily stops it and lets you explore the results to that point. While the search is paused, the icon changes to a play button. Clicking that button resumes the search from the point where you paused it.

- Finalizing a search stops it before it completes, but retains the results to that point and so you can view and explore it in the search view.

- In contrast, canceling a search stops it running, discards the results, and clears them from the screen.

The **Job inspector** icon takes you to the **Job inspector** page, which shows details about your search, such as the execution costs of your search, debug messages, and search job properties.

Use the **Save** menu to save the search, save the results, or save and share the results. If you save the search, you can find it on the **Searches & Reports** menu. If you save the results, you can review them by clicking on **Jobs** in the upper right corner of the screen.

Use the **Create** menu to create dashboards, alerts, reports, event types, and scheduled searches. We'll explain those in detail in Chapter 5.

Moving down to the upper left corner of the **Results** area, you see the following row of icons.

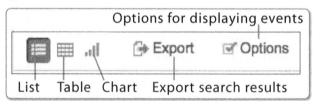

Figure 3-6. Results area icons

By default, Splunk shows events as a list, from most recent events to least, but you can click on the Table icon to view your results as a table, or you can click the Chart icon to view them as a chart. The Export button exports your search results in various formats: CSV, raw events, XML, or JSON.

Events? Results? What's the Difference?

Technically speaking, retrieved events from your indexes are called "events." If those events are transformed or summarized so that there is no longer a one-to-one mapping with events on disk, they are properly called "results." For example, a web-access event retrieved from a search is an event, but the top URL visited today is a result. That said, we are not going to be that picky, and will use the two terms interchangeably.

SPL™: Search Processing Language

Splunk helps sift data from the mass of indexed events into a form that is useful for answering real-world questions.

Figure 3-7 illustrates a common search pattern: retrieve events and generate a report. This search returns the top users in syslog errors.

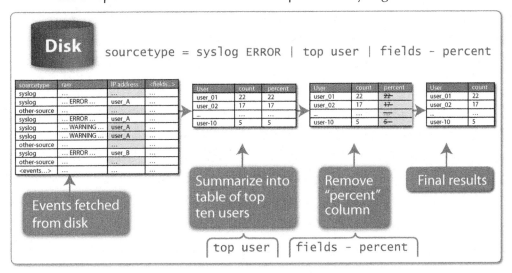

Figure 3-7. How a simple Splunk search is processed

The entire string

```
sourcetype=syslog ERROR | top user | fields - percent
```

is called a search, and the pipe character (|) separates the individual commands that make up the search.

Pipes

The first keyword after the pipe is the name of the search command. In this case the commands are `top` and `fields`. What command is retrieving the events from the index? Well, there is an implied command called search, at the beginning of any search that doesn't start with a pipe character. So, really, there are three search commands in the above search: search, top, and fields.

The results from each command are passed as input to the next command. If you have ever used a Linux shell such as bash, this concept is probably familiar.

Implied AND

sourcetype=syslog ERROR tells the search command to retrieve only events that have a sourcetype equal to syslog AND contain the term ERROR.

top user

The next command, top, returns the most common values of the specified fields. By default, top returns the top 10 most common values for the specified field, in descending order (thank you, David Letterman). In this case, the specified field is user, so top returns the users that appear most often in syslog events that contain the term ERROR. The output of top is a table of 3 columns (user, count, and percent), with 10 rows of values.

It's also important to understand that the output of the top command becomes the input to the next command after the pipe. In this sense, top has transformed the search results to a smaller set of values, which are further refined by the next command.

fields – percent

The second command, fields, with an argument of – percent, tells Splunk to remove the percent column from the output of the top command.

Exploratory Data Analysis: Spelunking with Splunk

What if you don't know anything about the data? Get creative and explore. You can do a search for "" to retrieve all events and then learn about them: look at some events, extract some interesting looking fields, get a top of that field, see how the events are broken up, perhaps derive some new fields based on other fields, cluster your results, see how one field varies with another field, and so on. (For more tips about learning what's in a source that you have little knowledge about, refer to http://splunk.com/goto/book#mining_tips.)*

Before we dive into the search commands in Chapter 4, let's cover the search command itself: a very special command that is critical for using Splunk.

The search Command

The search command is the workhorse of Splunk. It's one of the simplest and most powerful commands. It's such a basic command that you don't even need to type it anywhere before the first pipe, because it is invoked implicitly at the head of a search, retrieving events from the indexes on disk.

Not all searches retrieve data from Splunk indexes. For example, the inputcsv *command reads data from a CSV file. To enter commands of this sort as the first command, precede them with the pipe character. For example:* | inputcsv myfile.csv

---

When it's not the first command in a search, the search command can filter a set of results of the previous search. To do this, use the search command like any other command—with a pipe character followed by an explicit command name. For example, the command error | top url | search count>=2 searches for events on disk that have the word error, finds the top URLs, and filters any URLs that only occur once. In other words, of the 10 error events that top returns, show me only the ones where there are two or more instances of that URL.

Table 3-1 shows a few examples of implicit calls to the search command and their results.

Table 3-1. Implicit search commands

Search Arguments	Result
(warn OR error) NOT fail*	Retrieves all events containing either "warn" or "error", but not those that have "fail", "fails", "failed", "failure", etc.
"database error" fatal disk	Retrieves all events containing the phrase "database error", "fatal", and "disk" (the AND is implied).
host=main_web_server delay>2	Retrieves all events that have a host field with a value of main_web_server and a delay field with a value greater than 2.

Tips for Using the search Command

Here are a few tips for using the search command. They apply to many other commands as well.

Case-sensitivity

Keyword arguments to the search command are not case-sensitive, but field names are. (See Appendix B for more details about case-sensitivity.)

Using quotation marks in a search

You need quotation marks around phrases or field values that contain breaking characters such as whitespace, commas, pipes, square brackets, and equals signs. So, host=web09 is fine, but if the host value has spaces, for example, you'll need quotes around the value, as in host="webserver #9". In addition, to search for reserved keywords (e.g., AND, OR, NOT, etc.), use quotes.

To search for quotes use a backslash to escape the quote character. To find the phrase—*Splunk changed "life itself" for me*—you'd search for:

```
"Splunk changed \"life itself\" for me"
```

Boolean logic

Arguments—keywords and fields—to the search command are ANDed together, implicitly.

You can specify that either one of two or more arguments should be true using the OR keyword, in uppercase. OR has higher precedence than AND, so you can think of arguments using OR as having parentheses around them.

To filter out events that contain a particular word, use the NOT keyword.

Finally, you can use parentheses explicitly to make things more clear if you want to. For example, a search for x y OR z NOT w is the same as x AND (y OR z) AND NOT w.

Subsearches

The search command, like all commands, can be used as a subsearch—a search whose results are used as an argument to another search command. Subsearches are enclosed in square brackets. For example, to find all syslog events from the user that had the last login error, use the following command:

```
sourcetype=syslog [search login error | return user]
```

Here, a search for events having the terms `login` and `error` is performed, returning the first `user` value found, say `bob`, followed by a search for `sourcetype=syslog user=bob`.

If you're ready to continue your adventure in learning Splunk, Chapter 4 introduces you to more commands you will find immediately helpful.

4 SPL: Search Processing Language

In Chapter 3, we covered the most basic Splunk command in the SPL: search. This chapter describes some of the other SPL commands you'll want to learn.

This chapter takes a bare bones, learn-by-example approach to SPL commands. For complete reference documentation, see http://docs.splunk.com.

Table 4-1 summarizes the SPL commands covered in this chapter, by category.

Table 4-1. Common SPL Commands

Category	Description	Commands
Sorting Results	Ordering results and (optionally) limiting the number of results.	`sort`

Filtering Results	Taking a set of events or results and filtering them into a smaller set of results.	`search`
		`where`
		`dedup`
		`head`
		`tail`

Grouping Results	Grouping events so you can see patterns.	`transaction`

Reporting Results	Taking search results and generating a summary for reporting.	`top/rare`
		`stats`
		`chart`
		`timechart`

Filtering, Modifying, and Adding Fields	Filtering out (removing) some fields to focus on the ones you need, or modifying or adding fields to enrich your results or events.	`fields`
		`replace`
		`eval`
		`rex`
		`lookup`

Sorting Results

Sorting results is the province of the (you guessed it!) sort command.

sort

The sort command sorts search results by the specified fields.

Table 4-2 shows some examples.

Shorthand for Part of a Search

If we show just part of a series of commands (as we do in Table 4-2), you'll see:

> ... |

This means that some search preceded this command, but we are focusing on what comes afterward.

Table 4-2. `sort` Command Examples

Command	Result
... | sort 0 field1	Sort results in ascending order by field1, returning all results (0 means return them all; don't stop at 10,000, which is the default).
... | sort field1,-field2	Sort results by field1 in ascending order, and then by field2 in descending order, returning up to 10,000 results (the default).
... | sort 100 –field1,+field2	Sort results in descending order by field1, and then in ascending order by field2, returning the first 100 sorted results.
... | sort filename ... | sort num(filename) ... | sort str(filename)	Sort results by filename: • The first command lets Splunk decide how to sort the field values. • The second command tells Splunk to sort the values numerically. • The third command tells Splunk to sort the values lexicographically.

Hint: *Ascending order is the default for search results. To reverse the order of results, use a minus sign in front of a field used to order the results.*

Figure 4-1 illustrates the second example. We'll sort by ascending prices and descending ratings. The first result is the cheapest item with the highest user rating.

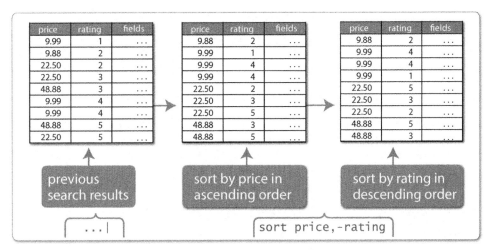

Figure 4-1. `sort` *Command*

Filtering Results

These commands take search results from a previous command and reduce them to a smaller set of results. In other words, you're narrowing
down your view of the data to show only the results you are looking for.

where

The `where` filtering command evaluates an expression for filtering results.
If the evaluation is successful and the result is TRUE, the result is retained;
otherwise, the result is discarded. For example:

```
source=job_listings | where salary > industry_average
```

This example retrieves jobs listings and discards those whose salary is not
greater than the industry average. It also discards events that are missing
either the `salary` field or the `industry_average` field.

This example compares two fields—`salary` and `industry_average`—
something we can only do with the `where` command. When comparing
field values to literal values, simply use the `search` command:

```
source=job_listings salary>80000
```

Table 4-3. where *Command Examples*

Command	Result
... | where distance/time > 100	Keep results whose distance field value divided by the time field value is greater than 100.
... | where like(src, "10.9.165.%") OR cidrmatch("10.9.165.0/25", dst)	Keep results that match the IP address or are in the specified subnet.

Figure 4-2 illustrates the command where distance/time > 100.

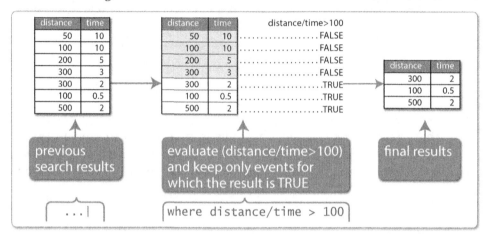

Figure 4-2. where *Command Example*

Tips for Using where

Like the eval command, the where command works with a large set of expression evaluation functions (see Appendix E for a complete list).

dedup

Removing redundant data is the point of the dedup filtering command. This command removes subsequent results that match specified criteria. That is, this command keeps only the first count results for each combination of values of the specified fields. If count is not specified, it defaults to 1 and returns the first result found (which is usually the most recent).

Table 4-4. dedup *Command Examples*

Command	Result
dedup host	Keep the first result for each unique host.
dedup 3 source	Keep the first three results for each unique source.
dedup source sortby -delay	Keep the first result for each unique source after first sorting the results by the delay field in descending order. Effectively this keeps the result with the largest delay value for each unique source.
dedup 3 source,host	Keep the first three results for each unique combination of source and host values.
dedup source keepempty=true	Keep the first result for each unique source, also keeping those with no source field.

Figure 4-3 illustrates the command dedup 3 source.

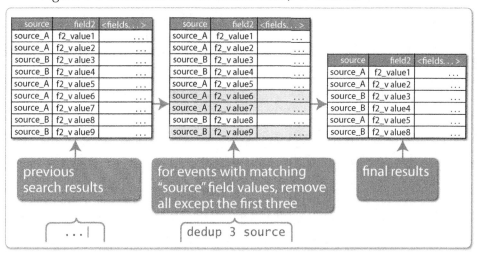

Figure 4-3. dedup *Command Example*

Key Points

- To keep all results but remove duplicate values, use the keepevents option.

- The results returned are the first results found with the combination of specified field values—generally the most recent ones. Use the sortby clause to change the sort order if needed.

- Fields where the specified fields do not all exist are retained by default. Use the `keepnull=<true/false>` option to override the default behavior, if desired.

head

The head filtering command returns the first count results. Using head permits a search to stop retrieving events from disk when it finds the desired number of results.

Heads or Tails?

The opposite of the head *command is the* tail *command, which returns the last results, rather than the first. The results are returned in reverse order, starting at the end of the results. Keep in mind that first is relative to the input order of events, which is usually in descending time order, meaning that, for example,* head 10 *returns the latest 10 events.*

Table 4-5. head Command Examples

Command	Result
... | head 5	Return the first 5 results.
... | head (action="startup")	Return the first events until we reach an event that does NOT have an action field with the value startup.

The first example in Table 4-5, head 5, is illustrated in Figure 4-4.

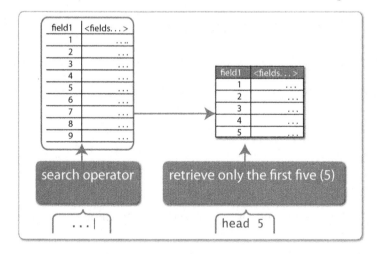

Figure 4-4. head Command Example

Grouping Results

The `transaction` command groups related events.

transaction

The `transaction` command groups events that meet various constraints into *transactions*—collections of events, possibly from multiple sources. Events are grouped together if all transaction definition constraints are met. Transactions are composed of the raw text (the `_raw` field) of each member event, the timestamp (the `_time` field) of the earliest member event, the union of all other fields of each member event, and some additional fields the describe the transaction such as `duration` and `event-count`.

Table 4-6. `transaction` *Command Examples*

Command	Result
`… | transaction clientip maxpause=5s`	Group events that share the same client IP address and have no gaps or pauses longer than five seconds.
	With this command, the search results may have multiple values for the `host` field. For example, requests from a single IP address could come from multiple hosts if multiple people are accessing the server from the same location.
`… | transaction clientip host maxspan=30s maxpause=5s`	Group events that share the same unique combination of client IP address and host, where the first and last events are no more than 30 seconds apart and no event in the transaction occurred no more than five seconds apart.
	In contrast with the first example, each result event has a distinct combination of the IP address (`clientip`) and host value within the limits of the time constraints. Therefore, you should not see different values of `host` or `clientip` addresses among the events in a single transaction.

`sourcetype=access*`
`action=purchase |`
`transaction clientip`
`maxspan=10m maxevents=3`
	Retrieve web access events that have an `action=purchase` value. These events are then grouped by the `transaction` command if they share the same `clientip`, where each session lasts no longer than 10 minutes and includes no more than three events.

`... | transaction JSES-`
`SIONID clientip`
`startswith="signon"`
`endswith="purchase" |`
`where duration>=1`
	Group events together that have the same session ID (`JSESSIONID`) and come from the same IP address (`clientip`) and where the first event contains the string, "`signon`" and the last event contains the string, "`pur-chase.`"
	
	The search defines the first event in the transaction as events that include the string, "`signon`", using the `startswith="signon"` argument. The `endswith="purchase"` argument does the same for the last event in the transaction.
	
	This example then pipes the transactions into the `where` command, which uses the `duration` field to filter out transactions that took less than a second to complete.

The second example in Table 4-6, `transaction clientip maxspan=30s maxpause=5s`, is illustrated in Figure 4-5.

Figure 4-5. `transaction` *Command Example*

Key Points

All the `transaction` command arguments are optional, but some constraints must be specified to define how events are grouped into transactions.

Splunk does not necessarily interpret the transaction defined by multiple fields as a conjunction (`field1 AND field2 AND field3`) or a disjunction (`field1 OR field2 OR field3`) of those fields. If there is a transitive relationship between the fields in the `<fields list>`, the `transaction` command uses it.

For example, if you searched for `transaction host cookie`, you might see the following events grouped into a single transaction:

```
event=1 host=a
event=2 host=a cookie=b
event=3 cookie=b
```

The first two events are joined because they have `host=a` in common and then the third is joined with them because it has `cookie=b` in common with the second event.

The transaction command produces two fields:

- `duration`: difference between the timestamps for the first and last events in the transaction.

- `eventcount`: number of events in the transaction.

Although the `stats` command (covered later in this section) and the `transaction` command both enable you to aggregate events, there is an important distinction:

- `stats` calculates statistical values on events grouped by the value of fields (and then the events are discarded).

- `transaction` groups events, and supports more options on how they are grouped and retains the raw event text and other field values from the original events.

Reporting Results

Reporting commands covered in this section include `top`, `stats`, `chart`, and `timechart`.

top

Given a list of fields, the `top` command returns the most frequently occurring tuple of those field values, along with their count and percentage. If you specify an optional by-clause of additional fields, the most frequent values for each distinct group of values of the by-clause fields are returned.

The opposite of top is rare

The opposite of the top *command is the* rare *command. Sometimes you want to know what is the least common value for a field (instead of the most common). The* rare *command does exactly that.*

Table 4-7. top *Command Examples*

Command	Result
... | top 20 url	Return the 20 most common URLs.
... | top 2 user by host	Return the top 2 user values for each host.
... | top user, host	Return the top 10 (default) user-host combinations.

The second example in Table 4-7, top 2 user by host, is illustrated in Figure 4-6.

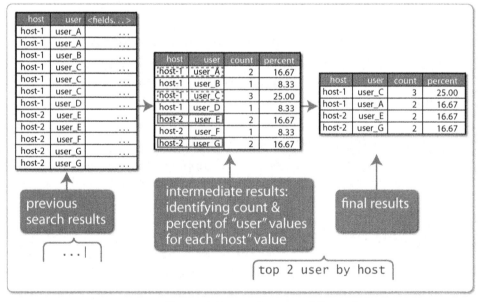

Figure 4-6. top *Command Example*

stats

The stats command calculates aggregate statistics over a dataset, similar to SQL aggregation. The resultant tabulation can contain one row, which represents the aggregation over the entire incoming result set, or a row for each distinct value of a specified by-clause.

There's more than one command for statistical calculations. The stats, chart, and timechart commands perform the same statistical calculations on your data, but return slightly different result sets to enable you to more easily use the results as needed.

- The stats command returns a table of results where each row represents a single unique combination of the values of the group-by fields.

- The chart command returns the same table of results, with rows as any arbitrary field.

- The timechart command returns the same tabulated results, but the row is set to the internal field, _time, which enables you to chart your results over a time range.

Table 4-8 shows a few examples of using the stats command.

What "as" means

Note: *The use of the keyword* as *in some of the commands in Table 4-14.* as *is used to rename a field. For example,* sum(price) *as "Revenue" means add up all the* price *fields and name the column showing the results "Revenue."*

Table 4-8. stats *Command Examples*

Command	Result
… | stats dc(host)	Return the distinct count (i.e., unique) of host values.
… | stats avg(kbps) by host	Return the average transfer rate for each host.
… | stats count(eval(method="GET")) as GET, count(eval(method="POST")) as POST by host	Return the number of different types of requests for each Web server (host). The resultant table contains a row for each host and columns for the GET and POST request method counts.
... | top limit=100 referer_domain | stats sum(count) as total	Return the total number of hits from the top 100 values of referer_domain.

`… | stats count,`
`max(Magnitude),`
`min(Magnitude),`
`range(Magnitude),`
`avg(Magnitude) by Region`
	Using USGS Earthquakes data, return the number of quakes and additional statistics, for each `Region`.

`… | stats values(product_type)`
`as Type, values(product_name)`
`as Name, sum(price) as "Rev-`
`enue" by product_id | re-`
`name product_id as "Prod-`
`uct ID" | eval Revenue="$`
`".tostring(Revenue,"commas")`
	Return a table with `Type`, `Name`, and `Revenue` columns for each `product_id` sold at a shop. Also, format the `Revenue` as $123,456.

The third example in Table 4-8, retrieving the number of GET and POST requests per host, is illustrated in Figure 4-7.

	host ⇕	GET ⇕	POST ⇕
1	apache1.splunk.com	1152	169
2	apache2.splunk.com	3771	154
3	apache3.splunk.com	3855	176

Figure 4-7. `stats` *Command Example*

Table 4-9 lists statistical functions that you can use with the `stats` command. (These functions can also be used with the `chart` and `timechart` commands, which are discussed later.)

Table 4-9. `stats` *Statistic al Functions*

Mathematical Calculations	
`avg(X)`	Returns average of the values of field X; see also, `mean(X)`.
`count(X)`	Returns the number of occurrences of the field X; to indicate a field value to match, format the X argument as an expression: `eval(field="value")`.
`dc(X)`	Returns the count of distinct values of field X.
`max(X)`	Returns the maximum value of field X. If the values are non-numeric, the max is determined per lexicographic ordering.
`median(X)`	Returns the middle-most value of field X.
`min(X)`	Returns the minimum value of field X. If the values are non-numeric, the min is determined per lexicographic ordering.

mode(X)	Returns the most frequent value of field X.
perc<percent-num>(X)	Returns the <percent-num>-th value of field X; for example, perc5(total) returns the 5th percentile value of the total field.
range(X)	Returns the difference between the max and min values of field X, provided values are numeric.
stdev(X)	Returns the sample standard deviation of field X. You can use wildcards when you specify the field name; for example, "*delay", which matches both "delay" and "xdelay".
sum(X)	Returns the sum of the values of field X.
var(X)	Returns the sample variance of field X.
Value Selections	
first(X)	Returns the first value of field X; opposite of last(X).
last(X)	Returns the last value of field X; opposite of first(X). Generally, a field's last value is the most chronologically oldest value.
list(X)	Returns the list of all values of field X as a multivalue entry. The order of the values matches the order of input events.
values(X)	Returns a list (as a multivalue entry) of all distinct values of field X, ordered lexicographically.
timechart only (not applicable to chart or stats)	
per_day(X)	Returns the rate of field X per day
per_hour(X)	Returns the rate of field X per hour
per_minute(X)	Returns the rate of field X per minute
per_second(X)	Returns the rate of field X per year

Note: All functions except those in the timechart only category are applicable to the chart, stats, and timechart commands.

chart

The chart command creates tabular data output suitable for charting. You specify the x-axis variable using over or by.

Table 4-10 shows a few simple examples of using the chart command; for more realistic scenarios, see Chapter 6.

Table 4-10. chart *Command Examples*

Command	Result
... | chart max(delay) over host	Return max(delay) for each value of host.
... | chart max(delay) by size bins=10	Chart the maximum delay by size, where size is broken down into a maximum of 10 equal-size buckets.
... | chart eval(avg(size)/ max(delay)) as ratio by host user	Chart the ratio of the average (mean) size to the maximum delay for each distinct host and user pair.
... | chart dc(clientip) over date_hour by category_id usenull=f	Chart the number of unique clientip values per hour by category. usenull=f excludes fields that don't have a value.
... | chart count over Magnitude by Region useother=f	Chart the number of earthquakes by Magnitude and Region. Use the useother=f argument to not output an "other" value for rarer Regions.
... | chart count(eval(method="GET")) as GET, count(eval(method="POST")) as POST by host	Chart the number of GET and POST page requests that occurred for each Web server (host)

Figures 4-8 (tabulated results) and 4-9 (bar chart on a logarithmic scale) illustrate the results of running the last example in Table 4-10:

	host ⬍	GET ⬍	POST ⬍
1	apache1.splunk.com	1152	169
2	apache2.splunk.com	3771	154
3	apache3.splunk.com	3855	176

Figure 4-8. chart *Command Example—Tabulated Results*

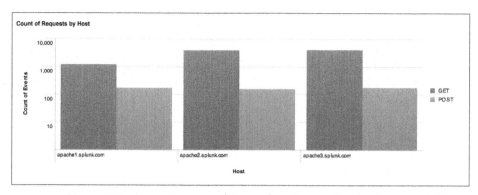

Figure 4-9. chart *Command Example—Report Builder Formatted Chart*

timechart

The timechart command creates a chart for a statistical aggregation applied to a field against time as the x-axis.

Table 4-11 shows a few simple examples of using the timechart command. Chapter 6 offers more examples of using this command in context.

Table 4-11. timechart *Command Example*

Command	Result
... | timechart span=1m avg(CPU) by host	Chart the average value of CPU usage each minute for each host.
... | timechart span=1d count by product-type	Chart the number of purchases made daily for each type of product. The span=1d argument buckets the count of purchases over the week into daily chunks.
...| timechart avg(cpu_seconds) by host | outlier	Chart the average cpu_seconds by host and remove outlying values that may distort the timechart's y-axis.
...| timechart per_hour(price) by product_name	Chart hourly revenue for the products that were purchased yesterday. The per_hour() function sums the values of the price field for each item (product_name) and scales that sum appropriately depending on the timespan of each bucket.

... | timechart count(eval(method="GET")) as GET, count(eval(method="POST")) as POST	Chart the number of page requests over time. The count() function and eval expressions are used to count the different page request methods, GET and POST.
... | timechart per_ hour(eval(method="GET")) as Views, per_ hour(eval(action="purchase")) as Purchases	For an ecommerce website, chart per_hour the number of produc t views and purchases—answering the question, how many views did not lead to purchases?

The fourth example in Table 4-11, charting hourly revenues by product name, is illustrated in figures 4-10 and 4-11.

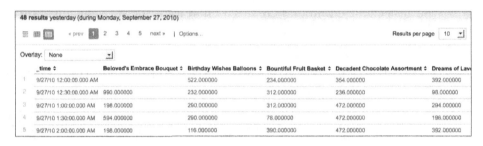

Figure 4-10. timechart *Command Example—Tabulated Results*

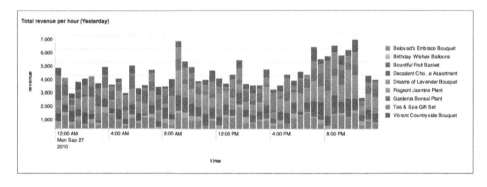

Figure 4-11. timechart *Command Example—Formatted Timechart*

Filtering, Modifying, and Adding Fields

These commands help you get only the desired fields in your search results. You might want to simplify your results by using the fields command to remove some fields. You might want to make your field values more readable for a particular audience by using the `replace` command. Or you might need to add new fields with the help of commands such as `eval`, `rex`, and `lookup`:

- The `eval` command calculates the value of a new field based on other fields, whether numerically, by concatenation, or through Boolean logic.

- The `rex` command can be used to create new fields by using regular expressions to extracting patterned data in other fields.

- The `lookup` command adds fields based on looking at the value in an event, referencing a lookup table, and adding the fields in matching rows in the lookup table to your event.

These commands can be used to create new fields or they can be used to overwrite the values of existing fields. It's up to you.

fields

The `fields` command removes fields from search results. Typical commands are shown in Table 4-6.

Table 4-12. `fields` *Command Examples*

Command	Result
... | fields - field1, field2	Remove `field1` and `field2` from the search results.
... | fields field1 field2	Keep only `field1` and `field2`.
... | fields field1 error*	Keep only `field1` and all fields whose names begin with `error`.
... | fields field1 field2 | fields - _*	Keep only `field1` and `field2` and remove all internal fields (which begin with an underscore). (Note: Removing internal fields can cause Splunk Web to render results incorrectly and create other search problems.)

The first example in Table 4-12, `fields - field1, field2`, is illustrated in Figure 4-12.

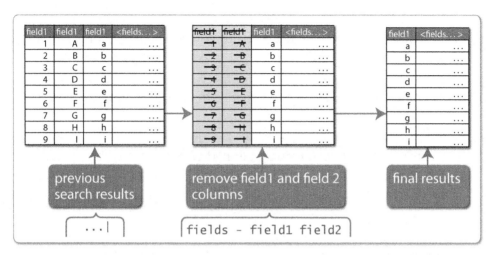

Figure 4-12. `fields` Command Example

Key Points

Internal fields, i.e., fields whose names start with an underscore, are unaffected by the `fields` command, unless explicitly specified.

replace

The `replace` command performs a search-and-replace of specified field values with replacement values.

The values in a search and replace are case-sensitive.

Table 4-13. `replace` Command Examples

Command	Result
`replace *localhost with loc-alhost in host`	Change any host value that ends with localhost to localhost.
`replace 0 with Critical , 1 with Error in msg_level`	Change msg_level values of 0 to Critical, and change msg_level values of 1 to Error.
`replace aug with August in start_month end_month`	Change any start_month or end_month value of aug to August.
`replace 127.0.0.1 with local-host`	Change all field values of 127.0.0.1 to localhost.

The second example in Table 4-13, `replace 0 with Critical , 1 with Error in msg_level`, is illustrated in Figure 4-13.

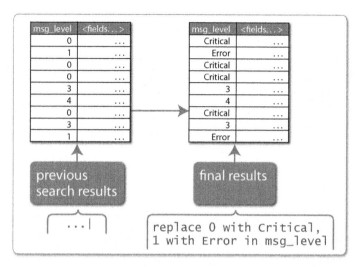

Figure 4-13. `replace` *Command Example*

eval

The `eval` command calculates an expression and puts the resulting value into a new field. The `eval` and `where` commands use the same expression syntax; Appendix E lists all the available functions.

Table 4-14. `eval` *Command Examples*

Command	Result
… | `eval velocity=distance/ time`	Set `velocity` to distance divided by time.
… | `eval status = if(error == 200, "OK", "Error")`	Set status to OK if error is 200; otherwise set status to Error.
… | `eval sum_of_areas = pi() * pow(radius_a, 2) + pi() * pow(radius_b, 2)`	Set sum_of_areas to be the sum of the areas of two circles.

Figure 4-14 illustrates the first example in Table 4-14, `eval velocity=distance/time`.

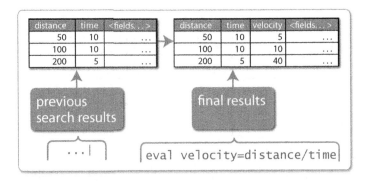

Figure 4-14. eval *Command Example*

The eval command results create a new velocity field. (If a velocity field exists, the eval command updates its value.) The eval command creates or overrides only one field at a time.

rex

The rex command extracts fields whose value matches a specified Perl Compatible Regular Expression (PCRE). (rex is shorthand for regular expression.)

What Are Regular Expressions?

Think of regular expressions as "wildcards on steroids." You've probably looked for files with expressions like *.doc or *.xls. Regular expressions let you take that to a whole new level of power and flexibility. If you're familiar with regular expressions, you're probably not reading this box. To learn more, see http://www.regular-expressions.info *—easily the best site on the topic.*

Table 4-15. rex *Command Examples*

Command	Result
… | rex "From: (?<from>.*) To: (?<to>.*)"	Extract from and to fields using regular expressions. If a raw event contains "From: Susan To: Bob", then from=Susan and to=Bob.
rex field=savedsearch_id (?<user>\w+);(?<app>\w+); (?<SavedSearchName>\w+)	Extract user, app, and SavedSearch-Name from a field called saved-search_id. If savedsearch_id = "bob;search;my_saved_search", then user=bob, app=search, and SavedSearchName=my_saved_search.

rex mode=sed "s/(\\\\d{4}-){3}/ XXXX-XXXX-XXXX-/g"	Use sed syntax to match the regex to a series of numbers, and replace them with an anonymized string.

Figure 4-15 illustrates the first example in Table 4-15, extracting from and to fields.

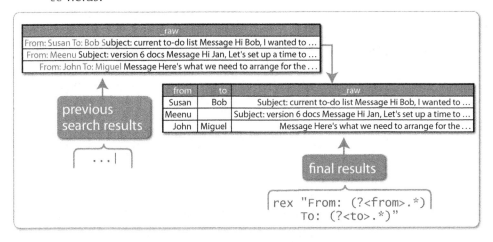

Figure 4-15. rex Command Example

lookup

The lookup command manually invokes field lookups from a lookup table, enabling you to add field values from an external source. For example, if you have 5-digit zip codes, you might do a lookup on the street name to apply a ZIP+4 9-digit zip code.

Table 4-16. Command Examples

Command	Result
... | lookup usertogroup user as local_user OUTPUT group as user_group	For a lookup table with fields user and group, specified in stanza name usertogroup in transform.conf,[1] look up the value of each event's local_user field. For entries that match, the value of the lookup table's group field is written to the event's user_group field.

---

[1]   Lookup tables can be configured through Manager » Lookups.

... | lookup dnslookup host OUTPUT ip	Given a field lookup named dns-lookup, referencing a Python script that performs a reverse DNS lookup and accepts either a host name or IP address as arguments, match the host name values (host field in your events to the host name values in the table, and then add the corresponding IP address values to your events (in the ip field).
... | lookup local=true user-ziplookup user as local_user OUTPUT zip as user_zip	For a local lookup table that is present only in the search head, look up the value of each event's user field. For entries that match, the value of the lookup table's zip field is written to the event's user_zip field.

Figure 4-16 illustrates the first example in Table 4-16, lookup userto-group user as local_user OUTPUT group as user_group.

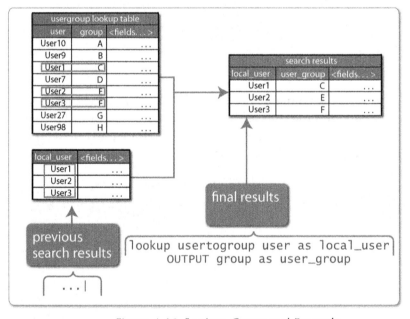

Figure 4-16. lookup *Command Example*

This chapter has provided a crash course in the commands in the SPL. The next chapter describes how you can enrich your data with tags and event types and tell Splunk to watch for certain patterns and alert you about them.

5 Enriching Your Data

To make your data more useable, add knowledge to it. What do we mean by that? When you tell Splunk how to extract fields from your data, you can start reasoning about those fields and give Splunk the knowledge to classify your data for deeper analysis. When you save reports and dashboards, your data becomes easier to understand for you and others. And when you create alerts, Splunk proactively reveals potential issues so that you don't have to look for them manually after the fact.

This chapter covers three areas:

* **Using Splunk to Understand Data** shows how to explore, categorize, and become familiar with your data.
* **Displaying Data** shows the basics of visualizing data.
* **Creating Alerts about Potential Problems** shows how to track and send alerts when metrics cross thresholds.

Using Splunk to Understand Data

When you first encounter a new source of machine data, it can look like a mess of meaningless numbers and cryptic text. The more you know about the system pumping out machine data, however, the more the data will make sense to you. But even if you know a data set well, further exploration can still bring new insights.

The first step in getting to know data is using Splunk to identify fields in the data. You can think of this like looking at all the pieces in a puzzle, first noticing their shapes. The next step is to categorize data as a preamble to aggregation and reporting. This is like sorting the puzzle pieces into border pieces and interior pieces. The more you are able to understand the data and piece the puzzle together, the clearer the picture becomes. At last, the picture is complete (displaying the data) and you can share it with others.

Identifying Fields: Looking at the Pieces of the Puzzle

Splunk recognizes many common types of data, referred to as *source types*. If you set the right source type, Splunk can use preconfigured settings to try to identify fields. This is the case with most types of web server logs, for example.

But there are often hidden attributes embedded in machine data. For example, a product category may be part of a URL. By examining events that have certain product categories in their URLs, you can determine response times and error rates for different sections of the site or information about which products are viewed the most.

Automatic Field Discovery

When you search, Splunk automatically extracts fields by identifying common patterns in the data, such as the presence of an equal sign (=) between a key and a value. For example, if an event contains "... `id=11 lname=smith` ... " Splunk automatically creates `id` and `lname` fields that have the example values. And, as mentioned in Chapter 2, some fields (such as `source`, `sourcetype`, `host`, `_time`, and `linecount`) are always identified.

Don't see what you're looking for? Start searching for it. Splunk displays only a certain number of fields in the UI by default. Hundreds more may be extracted perfectly. Searching for them brings them to the top.

The **Field Discovery** switch on the **Fields** sidebar in the UI turns this behavior on and off. You can see some selected fields (fields that Splunk selected by default or that you have selected), followed by fields that Splunk pulled out because they appeared in multiple events. If you click **Edit**, Splunk lists more fields that you can add to the group of selected fields. Clicking any field shows you the top values extracted from your search results.

For more information on automatic field extraction, see http://splunk.com/goto/book#auto_fields.

Configuring Field Extraction

Configuring field extraction can happen in two ways. You can let Splunk automate the configuration for you by using the Interactive Field Extractor, or you can manually specify the configuration yourself.

The Interactive Field Extractor

From any event in your search results, you can start the **Interactive Field Extractor** (IFX) by selecting **Extract Fields** from the **Event options** menu, which you reach by clicking the down arrow to the left of an event in the events list (see Figure 5-1).

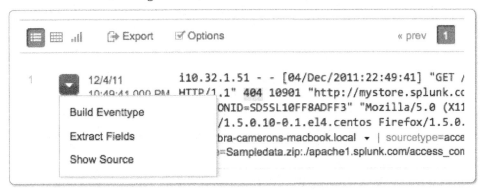

*Figure 5-1. Choosing **Extract Fields** from the **Event Options** menu starts the Interactive Field Extractor*

The IFX appears in another tab or window in your browser. By entering the kinds of values you seek (such as a client IP address in web logs), Splunk generates a regular expression that extracts similar values (this is especially helpful for the regular expression-challenged among us). You can test the extraction (to make sure it finds the field you're looking for) and save it with the name of the field.

To learn more about the Interactive Field Extractor, see http://splunk.com/goto/book#ifx.

Manually Configuring Field Extraction

From **Manager » Fields » Field extractions**, you can manually specify regular expressions to extract fields, which is a more flexible but advanced method for extracting fields.

To learn about manually specifying regular expressions, see http://splunk.com/goto/book#config_fields.

Search Language Extraction

Another way to extract fields is to use search commands. The most common command for extracting data is the rex command, described in the last chapter. It takes a regular expression and extracts fields that match that expression.

Sometimes the command you use depends on the kind of data from which you're extracting fields. To extract fields from multiline tabular events (such as command-line output), use `multikv`, and to extract from XML and JSON data, use `spath` or `xmlkv`.

To learn about commands that extract fields, see http://splunk.com/goto/book#search_fields.

Exploring the Data to Understand its Scope

After fields are extracted, you can start exploring the data to see what it tells you. Returning to our analogy of the puzzle, you begin by looking for patterns. What pieces help define the borders of the puzzle? How else can you categorize the pieces? By shape or color?

The **Search dashboard**'s **Fields** sidebar gives you some immediate information about each field:

- The basic data type of the field, indicated by a character to the left of the field name ("a" is text and "#" is numeric).

- The number of occurrences of the field in the events list (in parentheses following the fieldname).

When you click a field name in the **Fields** sidebar, a summary of the field pops up, including top values and links to additional charts.

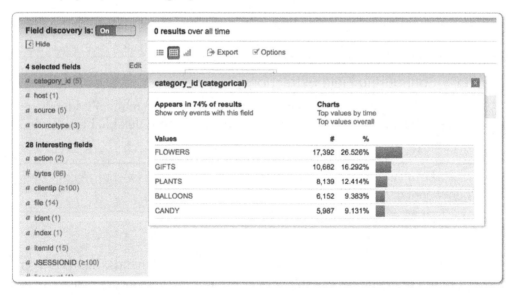

Figure 5-2. View a field summary by clicking on a field name in the **Fields** sidebar.

You can also narrow the events list to see only events that have a value for that field.

Exploring data using top

The `top` command gives you the most common field values, defaulting to the top ten. You can use the top command to answer questions like these:

- What are my top 10 web pages?

  ```
  sourcetype="access*" | top uri
  ```

- Who are the top users for each host?

  ```
  sourcetype="access*" | top user by host
  ```

- What are the top 50 source and destination IP pairs?

  ```
  ...| top limit=50 src_ip, dest_ip
  ```

Exploring data using stats

The `stats` command provides a wealth of statistical information about your data.

Here are a few simple ways to use it:

- How many 503 response errors[2] have I had?

  ```
  sourcetype="access*" status=503 | stats count
  ```

- What is the average kilobytes per second for each host?

  ```
  sourcetype="access*" | stats avg(kbps) by host
  ```

- How many people bought flowers yesterday? Use stats dc (distinct count) to ensure that each IP address is counted only once.

  ```
  sourcetype="access*" action=purchase category_id=flowers |
  stats dc(clientip)
  ```

- What is the 95th percentile of time the servers took to respond to web requests?

  ```
  sourcetype="access*" | stats perc95(spent)
  ```

Adding sparklines to the mix

As of Splunk 4.3, you can add simple line graphs, known as sparklines, to your tabular results. Sparklines let you quickly visualize a data pattern without creating a separate line chart.

For example, this search uses sparklines to show the number of events over time for each host:

```
* | stats sparkline count by host
```

---

[2]   A status of 503 in web server logs is a server-side error. The web server responded with a "service unavailable" message. The business meaning is that someone came to your site and didn't get through. It's time to look at operations if you keep seeing these errors.

Figure 5-3 shows sparklines in the table.

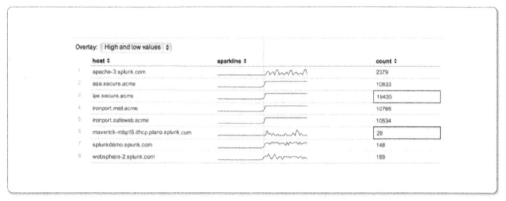

Figure 5-3. Sparklines show patterns in the data in the Events table

Here are a few more commands that demonstrate ways to use sparklines:

- What is the number of events for each status and category combination, over time?

```
sourcetype="access*" | stats sparkline count by status,
category_id
```

- What is the average time response time for each product category, over time?

```
sourcetype="access*" | stats sparkline(avg(spent)) by cat-
egory_id
```

Using a different data set (earthquake magnitude data), see how earthquake magnitude varies by region and over 6 hour chunks of time, with the more popular regions first.[3]

```
source=eqs7day-M2.5.csv | stats sparkline(avg(Magnitude),6h)
as magnitude_trend, count, avg(Magnitude) by Region | sort
count
```

Preparing for Reporting and Aggregation

After you have identified fields and explored the data, the next step is to start understanding what's going on. By grouping your data into categories, you can search, report, and alert on those categories.

The categories we are talking about are user-defined. You know your data, and you know what you want to get out of your data. Using Splunk, you can categorize your data as many ways as you like.

There are two primary ways that Splunk helps with categorizing data: tagging and event types.

---

[3]   We offer this as an example, but you can download real data and try it out by going to: http://earthquake.usgs.gov/earthquakes/catalogs/.

Tagging

Tags are an easy way to label any field value. If the host name `bdgpu-log-in-01` isn't intuitive, give it a tag, like `authentication_server`, to make it more understandable. If you see an outlier value in the UI and want to be able to revisit it later and get more context, you might label it `follow_up`.

To tag a field value in the events list, click the down arrow beside the field value you want to tag (see Figure 5-4).

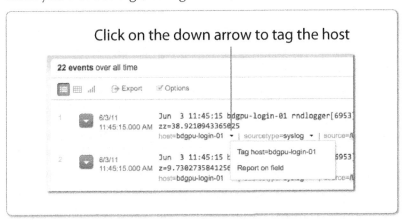

Figure 5-4. Tagging hosts

You can manage all your tags by going to **Manager » Tags**.

Let's suppose you've labeled your various host values with tags such as `webserver`, `database_server`, and so on. You can then report on those custom tags to see your data the way you want instead of how it happens to be named. Again, you decide how you want to look at your data. For example, to compare how the various host types perform over time, run a search such as:

```
... | timechart avg(delay) by tag::host
```

Reporting and the Joy of Negative Searching

From the moment you start looking at data, you should be thinking about reporting. What would you like to know about the data? What are you looking for? What "noise" would you like to remove from the data so that you can easily find what you're looking for?

This last point bears further explanation as an example of something Splunk does very well that few if any other data analysis software can: negative searching.

It's often said that you can't prove a negative. You can't look everywhere and say, what I seek is not there. With Splunk you can do negative searching and in fact you should. The reason it's hard to see what's happening with log files, and many other types of data, is that so much of it is the same, sort of business-as-usual machine data. With Splunk you can categorize that uninteresting data and tell Splunk to show you only what's unusual or different. Show me what I haven't seen before. Some security experts use Splunk in just this way to identify anomalous events that could indicate an intrusion, for example. If they've seen it before, they give it a tag and exclude it from their search. After you do this for a while, if anything odd happens, you'll see it right away.

Event Types

When you search in Splunk, you start by retrieving events. You implicitly look for a particular kind of event by searching for it. You could say that you were looking for events of a certain type. That's how "event types" are used: they let you categorize events.

Event types facilitate event categorization using the full power of the `search` command, meaning you can use Boolean expressions, wildcards, field values, phrases, and so on. In this way, event types are even more powerful than tags, which are limited to field values. But, like tags, how your data is categorized is entirely up to you.

You might create event types to categorize events such as where a customer purchased, when a system crashed, or what type of error condition occurred.

It's all about what you need to know about your events.

Here are some ground rules for a search that defines an event type:

- No pipes. You can't have a pipe in a search used to create an event type (i.e., it cannot have any search commands other than the implied `search` command).

- No subsearches. At the end of Chapter 3, we briefly covered the wheel-within-a-wheel that is subsearches; for now, remember that you can't use them to create event types.

Here's a simple example. In our ongoing quest to improve our website, we're going to create four event types based on the `status` field:

- status="2*" is defined as *success*.

- status="3*" is defined as *redirect*.

- status="4*" is defined as *client_error*.

- status="5*" is defined as *server_error*.

To create the event type `success` as we've defined it, you would perform a search like this:

```
sourcetype="access*" status="2*"
```

Next, choose **Create » Event type**. The **Save As Event Type** dialog appears where you name the event type, optionally assign tags, and click **Save**.

*To see the event types matching your search results, click **eventtype** in the **Fields** sidebar. This multivalued field shows all the event types for the events in the events list.*

We create the other three event types in just the same way, and then run a `stats count` to see the distribution:

```
sourcetype="access*"| stats count by eventtype
```

The results look like Figure 5-5.

Figure 5-5. Breaking down events by event type

There are relatively few events with an event type of `server_error` but, nonetheless, they merit a closer look to see if we can figure out what they have in common.

Clicking `server_error` lets us to drill down into events of just that event type, where we see 15 events that all look something like the one shown in Figure 5-6.

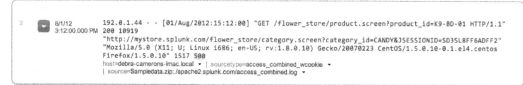

Figure 5-6. An event with a server error

The `server_error` events have one rather disturbing thing in common: people are trying to buy something when the server unavailable status occurs. In other words, this is costing us money! It's time to go talk to the person who administers that server and find out what's wrong.

Nesting Event Types

You can build more specific event types on top of more general event types. We could define a new event type `web_error` *with other event types as building blocks:*

> `eventtype=client_error OR eventtype=server_error`

Of course, you should use this sparingly because you don't want to risk losing track and inadvertently creating circular definitions.

Tagging Event Types

Event types can have tags (and so can any field value for that matter). For example, you can tag all error event types with the tag `error`. You can then add a more descriptive tag about the types of errors relevant to that event type. Perhaps there are three types of errors: one type that indicates early warnings of possible problems, others that indicate an outage that affects the user, and others that indicate catastrophic failure. You can add another tag to the error event types that is more descriptive, such as `early_warning`, `user_impact`, or `red_alert`, and report on them separately.

Together, event types and tags let you start building a higher-level model from the detailed events of the machine data in question. Usually, this is an iterative process. You begin by tagging a few useful fields, using them for monitoring and alerting. Soon after, you'll create a few event types to do more complex categorization. Perhaps you build higher-level event types by referencing lower-level event types. Perhaps you then add tags to your event types to unify several categorizations. All the while, you're adding knowledge to Splunk about how to organize and label your data for your needs.

Earlier we mentioned negative searching. If you tag all the event types you don't especially want to see with a tag of normal, *you can then search for events that are NOT normal. This brings abnormalities to the surface.*

```
NOT tag::eventtype=normal
```

Visualizing Data

So far we've shown you a couple of ways to get at data visualizations:

- Clicking a fieldname in the **Fields** sidebar to see some quick graphics about a field.
- Using the `top` and `stats` search commands.
- Using sparklines to see inline visualizations in the events table results.

This section shows you how to create charts and dashboards for visualizing your data.

Creating Visualizations

When you look at a table of data, you may see something interesting. Putting that same data into charts and graphs can reveal new levels of information and bring out details that are hard to see otherwise.

To create charts of your data, after you run a search, select **Create » Report**. Alternatively, in Splunk 4.3, click the **Results Chart** icon in the Results area to display a chart of your results.

Splunk offers various chart types: column, line, area, bar, pie, and scatterplots.

What product categories are affected most by 404 errors? This search calculates the number of events for each **category_id** and generates the pie chart shown in Figure 5-7.

```
sourcetype="access*" status="404" | stats count by catego-
ry_id
```

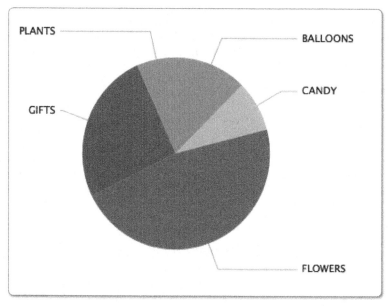

Figure 5-7. Pages not found by product category

Given that flowers and gifts are among the highest-margin products, we'd better add some redirects for the bad URLs (and try to get the sites that are linking to our pages to update their links).

When you mouse over any graphic in Splunk, you get more information about the data behind that portion of the graphic. See Figure 5-8.

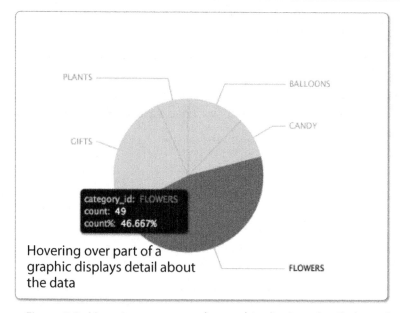

Figure 5-8. Hovering over part of a graphic displays detail about the data

Creating Dashboards

The end result of using Splunk for monitoring is usually a dashboard with several visualizations. A dashboard is made up of report panels, which can be a chart, a gauge, or a table or list of search results (often the data itself is interesting to view).

When designing dashboards, ask yourself, "Of all of these charts, which ones would I want to see first? Which ones would end users want to see first? Which ones would line-of-business managers want to see first?" Maybe each audience needs its own dashboard.

Then you can ask, "What questions arise from looking at this dashboard?" Splunk automatically handles many kinds of drill downs into chart specifics with a simple click on the chart. (Advanced users can specify drill-down behavior explicitly, but that is beyond the scope of this book.)

One key point to remember is that simple visualizations are generally the most popular with all levels of users. You can, and should, make more advanced and detailed dashboards, but make sure to do a good job covering the simple, high-level views.

Figure 5-9 shows an example of a dashboard.

Figure 5-9. A dashboard

The best way to build a dashboard is not from the top down but from the bottom up, with each panel. Start by using Splunk's charting capabilities to show the vital signs in various ways. When you have several individual charts showing different parts of the system's health, place them onto a dashboard.

Creating a Dashboard

In Splunk 4.3, to create a dashboard and add a report, chart, or search results to it:

1. Run a search that generates a report for a dashboard.

2. Select **Create » Dashboard panel**.

3. Give your search a name, and click **Next**.

4. Decide if you want this report to go on a new dashboard or on an existing dashboard. If you're creating a new dashboard, give it a name. Click **Next**.

5. Specify a title for your dashboard and a visualization (table, bar, pie, gauge, etc.), and when you want the report for the panel to run (whenever the dashboard is displayed or on a fixed schedule).

6. Click **Next** followed by the **View dashboard** link or **OK**.

Viewing a Dashboard

At any time you can view a dashboard by selecting it from the **Dashboards & Views** menu at the top of the page.

Editing a Dashboard

While viewing your dashboard, you can edit it by clicking **On** in the **Edit** mode selector and then clicking the **Edit** menu of any panel you want to edit. From there, you can edit the search that generates a report or how it's visualized, or delete the panel.

Creating Alerts

What is an alert? You can think of an alert as an "if-then" statement that gets evaluated on a schedule:

```
If this happens, then do that in response.
```

The "if" in this case is a search. The "then" is the action you want to be taken in response to the "if" clause being fulfilled.

More formally, an alert is a search that runs periodically with a condition evaluated on the search results. When the condition matches, some actions are executed.

Creating Alerts through a Wizard

To get started with creating an alert, the first step is to search for the condition about which you want to be alerted. Splunk takes whatever search is in the search bar when you create an alert and uses that as a saved search, which becomes the basis for your alert (the "if" in your "if-then").

With the search you want in the **search bar**, select **Create » Alert**. This starts a wizard that makes it easy to create an alert.

Scheduling an Alert

On the **Schedule** screen of the **Create Alerts dialog**, you name the alert and specify how you want Splunk to execute it.

You can choose whether Splunk monitors for a condition by running a search in real time, by running a scheduled search periodically, or by monitoring in real time over a rolling window.

Here are the use cases for these three options:

• Monitor in real time if you want to be alerted whenever the condition happens.

• Monitor on a scheduled basis for less urgent conditions that you nonetheless want to know about.

• Monitor using a real-time rolling window if you want to know if a certain number of things happen within a certain time period (it's a hybrid of the first two options in that sense). For example, trigger the alert as soon as you see more than 20 404s in a 5-minute window.

If you specify that you want to monitor on a schedule or in a rolling window, you must also specify the time interval and the number of results that should match the search to trigger the alert. Alternatively, you could enter a custom condition, which is a search that is executed if the alert condition is met. Custom conditions are described later in this chapter.

Figure 5-10. Scheduling an alert

The next step is to set limits and specify what to do if the alert is triggered.

Specifying Actions

What should happen if the alert condition occurs? On the **Action** screen of the **Create Alert** dialog, you specify what action or actions you want to take (sending email, running a script, showing triggered alerts in Alerts Manager).

In Figure 5-11, the user chose all of the above actions, letting us see all the options available here.

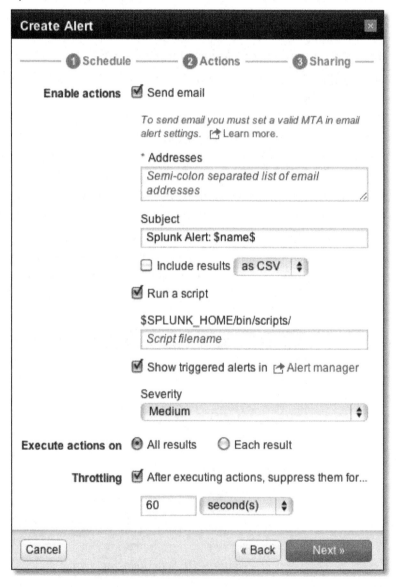

Figure 5-11. Action screen of the wizard

- **Send email.** Email has the following options:
    - ◊ Email addresses. Enter at least one.
    - ◊ Subject line. You can leave this as the default, which is Splunk Alert: AlertName. The alert name is substituted for $name$. (This means you could change that subject to: Oh no! $name$ happened.)
    - ◊ Include the results that triggered the alert. Click the checkbox to include them either as an attached CSV file or select **inline** to put them right into the email itself.
- **Run a script.** You specify the script name, which must be placed in Splunk's home directory, within /bin/scripts or within an app's / bin/scripts directory.
- **Show triggered alerts in Alert manager**, which you reach by clicking **Alerts** in the upper right corner of the UI.

After you choose an action (or two or three), you can fill in a few more options:

- Set the severity. The severity is metadata for your reference so that you can classify alerts. The levels are info, low, medium, high, and critical. Severity shows up in **Alert manager**.

- Execute actions on all results or each result. This determines whether Splunk takes the action (such as sending an email) for the group of results that matches the search or for each individual result. "All results" is the default.

- Throttling. Alerts are effective only if they tell you what you need to know when you need to know it. Too many alerts and you'll ignore them. Too few and you won't know what's happening. This option specifies how long Splunk should wait to perform the action associated with the alert again, after it has been triggered. If you specify a rolling window, the wizard defaults the throttling interval to match that window. More throttling options are described later in this chapter.

After you click **Next**, the final step is to specify whether the alert is private or shared for read-only access to users of the current app. Click **Finish** to finalize the alert.

Tuning Alerts Using Manager

Setting the right limits for alerting usually requires trial and error. It may take some adjustment to prevent too many unimportant alerts or too few important ones. The limits should be tuned so that, for example, one spike in an isolated vital sign doesn't trigger an alert, but 10 vital signs getting within 10% of their upper limits do.

It's easy to create alerts quickly using the wizard, but still more options for tuning alerts are available using Manager.

Remember that saved searches underlie alerts. As a result, you edit them like you would a saved search. To edit to your alert, choose **Manager** and then **Searches and Reports**.

Select a saved search from the list to display its parameters.

Setting Alert Conditions

Thinking of an alert as an If-Then statement, you have more flexibility on the If side by editing through the Manager. The alert can be set to trigger:

• Always

• Depending on the number of events, hosts, sources

• Custom condition

Although the wizard offered to alert on the number of events, here you have options for alerting by the number of hosts or sources. Consider hosts. It's one thing if you start seeing "server unavailable" status on one web server in a cluster, but it's quite another thing if you suddenly see it on more and more of your servers. Clearly there's a spike and the servers are not handling the traffic.

This screen offers more flexibility for defining the threshold for the alert:

• is greater than

• is less than

• is equal to

• not equal to

• rises by

• falls by

The first four options were exposed through the wizard, but here we add the ability to alert if the number rises or falls by a certain number or by a certain percentage (such as 50%). "rises by" and "falls by" allow you to effectively set alerts for conditions that are relative (it's often not the absolute number as much as a doubling or tripling that you want to be alerted about). "rises by" and "falls by" are not supported on conditions that use real-time searches.

Setting Custom Conditions

Although the UI offers flexibility for configuring the most common kinds of alert conditions, sometimes you need even more flexibility in the form of custom conditions.

A custom condition is a search against the results of the alert's main search. If it returns any results, the condition is true, and the alert is fired.

For example, you might want to be alerted anytime a host goes down, but exclude hosts that are undergoing scheduled maintenance. To do this, you'd make a main search to return all hosts that go down and a custom condition filters out "false positives"—hosts that are in the calendar for scheduled maintenance. In this way, you are alerted only if a host goes down unexpectedly.

Throttling Alerts

Splunk lets you tune alerts so that they tell you something meaningful. A message that tells you something important is helpful. One hundred messages, on the other hand, whether justified or not, is not helpful. It's noise.

Splunk lets you throttle alerts so that even if they are triggered, they go off only once in a particular time interval. In other words, if the first alert is like the first kernel of popcorn that pops, you don't want alerts for all those other kernels, which are really related to that first alert. (If popcorn had a second alert, it should go off just after all functional kernels pop and before any of them burn.)

This is what throttling does. You can tell Splunk to alert you but not to keep alerting you.

In the middle of the Manager's screen for editing alerts is an option called **Alert mode** (see Figure 5-12).

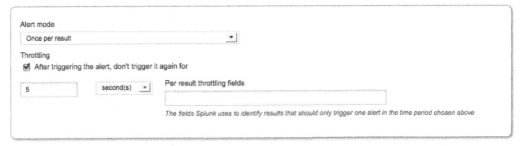

Figure 5-12. Alert Mode

You can be alerted once per search, that is, for all results, or you can be alerted once per result. Per result alerts can be further throttled by fields. For example, you may want to be alerted whenever the condition is fulfilled, but only once per host. Let's say that disk space is running low on a server and you want to be alerted when there's less than 30% free space available. If you specify host in **Per result throttling fields**, you would only be notified once for each host during the specified time period. If you were dealing with user login failures, you might enter username as the per-result-throttling field.

Customizing Actions for Alerting

By writing or modifying scripts, you can set up custom actions for alerts. For example, you may want an alert to:

- Send an SMS to the people who can help with the problem.
- Create a helpdesk ticket or other type of trouble ticket.
- Restart the server.

All alert actions are based on a script, including sending an email. So is creating an RSS feed. With that in mind, you can see that you can set up alert actions as flexibly as needed using scripting.

To learn more about creating custom alert scripts, see http://splunk.com/goto/book#custom_alerts

---

The Alerts Manager

Mission control for alerts is the **Alert manager**.

Click **Alert** in the upper right corner of the screen to display the **Alert manager**.

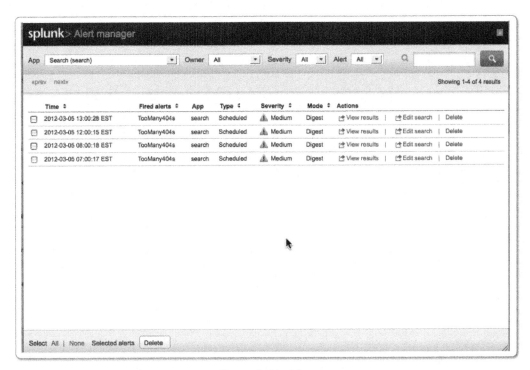

Figure 5-13. Alert manager

A brief clarification of terminology is needed here. We'll refer to the saved if-then scheduled search as an alert, and an individual firing of that alert as an alert instance.

The **Alert manager** shows the list of most recent firings of alerts (i.e., alert instances). It shows when the alert instance fired, and provides a link to view the search results from that firing and to delete the firing. It also shows the alert's name, app, type (scheduled, real-time, or rolling window), severity, and mode (digest or per-result). You can also edit the alert's definition.

PART II
RECIPES

6   Recipes for Monitoring and Alerting

The first five chapters of this book prepared you for using Splunk to solve problems, answer questions, and explore your data in new and interesting ways.

In this chapter, we'll present monitoring and alerting recipes. Monitoring refers to reports you can visually monitor and alerting refers to conditions monitored by Splunk, which can automatically trigger actions.

These recipes are meant to be brief solutions to common monitoring and alerting problems. Each recipe includes a problem statement followed by a description of how to use Splunk to solve the problem. Some of the more complex examples suggest variations on the recipe for you to explore.

To ask questions and find more answers like these, visit http://splunkbase.com.

Monitoring Recipes

Monitoring can help you see what is happening in your data. How many concurrent users are there? How are key metrics changing over time?

In addition to recipes that monitor various conditions, this section provides recipes that describe how to use search commands to extract fields from semi-structured and structured data.

Monitoring Concurrent Users

Problem

You need to determine how many concurrent users you have at any particular time. This can help you gauge whether some hosts are overloaded and enable you to better provision resources to meet peak demand.

Solution

First, perform a search to retrieve relevant events. Next, use the `concurrency` command to find the number of users that overlap. Finally, use the `timechart` reporting command to display a chart of the number of concurrent users over time.

Let's say you have the following events, which specify date, time, request duration, and username:

```
5/10/10 1:00:01 ReqTime=3 User=jsmith
5/10/10 1:00:01 ReqTime=2 User=rtyler
5/10/10 1:00:01 ReqTime=50 User=hjones
5/10/10 1:00:11 ReqTime=2 User=rwilliams
5/10/10 1:00:12 ReqTime=3 User=apond
```

You can see that, at 1:00:01, there are three concurrent requests (`jsmith`, `rtyler`, `hjones`); at 1:00:11, there are two (`hjones`, `rwilliams`); and at 1:00:12, there are three (`hjones`, `rwilliams`, `apond`).

Use this search to show the maximum concurrent users for any particular time:

```
<your search here> sourcetype=login_data
| concurrency duration=ReqTime
| timechart max(concurrency)
```

To learn more about the concurrency command, see http://splunk.com/goto/book#concurrency

---

Monitoring Inactive Hosts

Problem

You need to determine which hosts have stopped sending data. A host might stop logging events if the server, or application producing logs, has crashed or been shut down. This often indicates a serious problem. If a host stops logging events, you'll want to know about it.

Solution

Use the `metadata` command, which reports high-level information about hosts, sources, and source types in the Splunk indexes. This is what is used to create the Summary Dashboard. Note the pipe character is at the beginning of this search, because we're not retrieving events from a Splunk index, rather we're calling a data-generating command (`metadata`).

Use the following search to take the information on hosts, sort it so the least recently referenced hosts are first, and display the time in a readable time format:

```
| metadata type=hosts
| sort recentTime
| convert ctime(recentTime) as Latest_Time
```

You'll quickly see which hosts haven't logged data lately.

To learn more about the metadata command, see http://splunk.com/goto/book#metadata

---

Reporting on Categorized Data

Problem

You need to report on segments of your data that aren't neatly defined.

Solution

To search for specific parts of your data, classify your events using tags and event types. Tags are simpler but event types are more powerful (tags and event types are discussed in Chapter 5).

You might wonder how this categorization of data comes under monitoring. That's because when you categorize data using tags and event types, you not only categorize the data you have today, but you teach Splunk to categorize data like that every time it shows up. You are teaching Splunk to be on the lookout for data that has certain characteristics. Think of tags and event types like putting out an all points bulletin (APB) for your data.

Using Tags

You can classify simple field=value pairs using tags. For example, classify events that have host=db09 as a database host by tagging that field value. This creates a tag::host field having a value of database, on events with host=db09. You can then use this custom classification to generate reports.

Here are a couple of examples that use tags.

Show the top ten host types (good for bar or pie charts):

```
... | top 10 tag::host
```

Compare how the various host types perform over time:

```
... | timechart avg(delay) by tag::host
```

Using Event Types

When you use event types, instead of tags, to classify events, you are not limited to a simple field=value. You can use the full power of the `search` command, including Boolean operations, phrase matching, and wildcards. You could make an event type called `database_host` with a definition of "`host=db* OR host=orcl*`", and another event type called `web_host`. Repeat the same searches as you did for tags, but replace `tag::host` with `eventtype`. For example, to show the top ten event types:

```
... | top 10 eventtype
```

Because event types are not specific to a dimension, such as hosts, user type, or error codes, they are all in a common namespace, jumbled together. A search for `top eventtypes` might return `database_host` and `web_error`, which is probably not what you want because you'd be comparing apples to oranges. Fortunately you can filter which event types you report on, using the `eval` command, if you use a common naming convention for your event types.

As an example, using event types, compare how the various host types perform (displayed as a timechart), using only event types that end in `_host`:

```
...| eval host_types = mvfilter(match(eventtype, "_host$"))
    | timechart avg(delay) by host_types
```

Comparing Today's Top Values to Last Month's

Problem

You need to know the top N values today and how they compare to last month's values. This can answer questions like, which products, or database errors, are suddenly becoming more popular than they used to be?

Solution

For this solution, we'll use the example of music data to show the top 10 most played artists today and their average position for the month. Assume the events have an `artist` field and a `sales` field that tells how many units were sold at a particular time. We'll use the sum of `sales` as our metric—sum(`sales`)—but we could use any other metric.

The full search looks daunting at first, but you can break it down into simple steps:

1. Get the monthly rankings by artist.
2. Get the daily rankings by artist and append them to the results.

3. Use stats to join the monthly and daily rankings by artist.

4. Use sort and eval to format the results.

Get the monthly rankings

Use this search to find the 10 biggest monthly sales by artist:

```
sourcetype=music_sales earliest=-30d@d
| stats sum(sales) as month_sales by artist
| sort 10 - month_sales
| streamstats count as MonthRank
```

The `earliest=-30d@d` tells Splunk to retrieve events starting at 30 days ago (in other words, get events from the last month). `stats` calculates the sums of sales for each artist as the `month_sales` field. You now have a row for each artist, with two columns: `month_sales` and `artist`. `sort 10 - month_sales` keeps only those rows with the ten largest `month_sales` values, in sorted order from largest to smallest. The `streamstats` command adds one or more statistics to each event, based on the current value of the aggregate at the time the event is seen (not on the results as a whole, like the `stats` command does). Effectively, `streamstats count as MonthRank` assigns the first result `MonthRank=1`, the second result `MonthRank=2`, and so on.

Get yesterday's rankings

Make three small changes to the monthly-rankings search to get yesterday's rank:

- Change the value for `earliest` from `-30d@d` to `-1d@d` to get the rankings from yesterday.

- Change every instance of "month" in the search to "day".

- Wrap the search in an `append` command so that the results are appended to the results from the first search.

```
append [
  search sourcetype=music_sales earliest=-1d@d
  | stats sum(sales) as day_sales by artist
  | sort 10 - day_sales
  | streamstats count as DayRank
]
```

Use stats to join the monthly and daily ranks by artist

Use the `stats` command to join the results by artist, putting the first monthly and daily rankings into one result.

```
stats first(MonthRank) as MonthRank first(DayRank) as
DayRank by artist
```

Format the output

Finally, we'll calculate the difference in ranking between the monthly and daily rank, sort the results by the daily rank, and display the fields in music billboard order (rank, artist, change in rank, old rank):

```
eval diff=MonthRank-DayRank
| sort DayRank
| table DayRank, artist, diff, MonthRank
```

Summary

Putting it all together, the search is as follows:

```
sourcetype=music_sales earliest=-30d@d
| stats sum(sales) as month_sales by artist
| sort 10 - month_sales | streamstats count as MonthRank
| append [
  search sourcetype=music_sales earliest=-1d@d
    | stats sum(sales) as day_sales by artist
    | sort 10 - day_sales | streamstats count as DayRank
  ]
| stats first(MonthRank) as MonthRank first(DayRank) as
DayRank by artist
| eval diff=MonthRank-DayRank
| sort DayRank
| table DayRank, artist, diff, MonthRank
```

Variations

Here, we used the sum of sales as our metric—sum(sales)—but we could use any metric, such as min(sales), or change the time ranges to compare last week to this week.

To learn more about the streamstats command, see http://splunk.com/goto/book#streamstats

---

Finding Metrics That Fell by 10% in an Hour

Problem

You want to know about metrics that have dropped by 10% in the last hour. This could mean fewer customers, fewer web page views, fewer data packets, and the like.

Solution

To see a drop over the past hour, we'll need to look at results for at least the past two hours. We'll look at two hours of events, calculate a separate metric for each hour, and then determine how much the metric has changed between those two hours. The metric we're looking at is the count of the number of events between two hours ago and the last hour. This search compares the count by host of the previous hour with the current hour and filters those where the count dropped by more than 10%:

```
earliest=-2h@h latest=@h
| stats count by date_hour,host
| stats first(count) as previous, last(count) as current by
host
| where current/previous < 0.9
```

The first condition (`earliest=-2h@h latest=@h`) retrieves two hours worth of data, snapping to hour boundaries (e.g., 2-4pm, not 2:01-4:01pm). We then get a count of the number of those events per hour and host. Because there are only two hours (two hours ago and one hour ago), `stats first(count)` returns the count from two hours ago and `last(count)` returns the count from one hour ago. The `where` clause returns only those events where the current hour's count is less than 90% of the previous hour's count (which shows that the percentage dropped 10%).

As an exercise for you, think about what will go wrong with this search when the time span crosses midnight. Do you see how to correct it by adding `first(_time)` to the first `stats` command and sorting by that new value?

Variations

Instead of the number of events, use a different metric, such as the average delay or minimum bytes per second, and consider different time ranges, such as day over day.

Charting Week Over Week Results

Problem

You need to determine how this week's results compare with last week's.

Solution

First, run a search over all the events and mark whether they belong to this week or last week. Next, adjust the time value of last week's events to look like this week's events (so they graph over each other on the same time range). Finally create a chart.

Let's get results from the last two weeks, snapped to the beginning of the week:

```
earliest=-2w@w latest=@w
```

Mark events as being from this week or last week:

```
eval marker = if (_time < relative_time(now(), "-1w@w"),
                  "last week", "this week")
```

Adjust last week's events to look like they occurred this week:

```
eval _time = if (marker=="last week",
                 _time + 7*24*60*60, _time)
```

Chart the desired metric, using the week marker we set up, such as a timechart of the average bytes downloaded for each week:

```
timechart avg(bytes) by marker
```

This produces a timechart with two labeled series: "last week" and "this week".

Putting it all together:

```
earliest=-2w@w latest=@w
| eval marker = if (_time < relative_time(now(), "-1w@w"),
                    "last week", "this week")
| eval _time  = if (marker=="last week",
  _time + 7*24*60*60, _time)
| timechart avg(bytes) by marker
```

If you use this pattern often, you'll want to save it as a macro to reuse it.

Variations

Explore different time periods, such as day over day, with different chart types. Try different charts other than avg(bytes). Alternatively, remove the snapping to week boundaries by setting earliest=-2w, not using a latest value (it defaults to "now"), and changing the relative_time() argument to -1w.

Identify Spikes in Your Data

Problem

You want to identify spikes in your data. Spikes can show you where you have peaks (or troughs) that indicate that some metric is rising or falling sharply. Traffic spikes, sales spikes, spikes in the number of returns, spikes in database load—whatever type of spike you are interested in, you want to watch for it and then perhaps take some action to address those spikes.

Solution

Use a moving trendline to help you see the spikes. Run a search followed by the `trendline` command using a field you want to create a trendline for.

For example, on web access data, we could chart an average of the `bytes` field:

```
sourcetype=access* | timechart avg(bytes) as avg_bytes
```

To add another line/bar series to the chart for the simple moving average (sma) of the last 5 values of `bytes`, use this command:

```
trendline sma5(avg_bytes) as moving_avg_bytes
```

If you want to clearly identify spikes, you might add an additional series for spikes—when the current value is more than twice the moving average:

```
eval spike=if(avg_bytes > 2 * moving_avg_bytes, 10000, 0)
```

The 10000 here is arbitrary and you should choose a value relevant to your data that makes the spike noticeable. Changing the formatting of the Y-axis to Log scale also helps.

Putting this together our search is:

```
sourcetype=access*
| timechart avg(bytes) as avg_bytes
| trendline sma5(avg_bytes) as moving_avg_bytes
| eval spike=if(avg_bytes > 2 * moving_avg_bytes, 10000, 0)
```

Variations

We used a simple moving average for the last 5 results (sma5). Consider a different number of values (for example, sma20), and other moving average types, such as exponential moving average (ema) and weighted moving average (wma).

Alternatively, you can bypass the charting altogether and replace the above `eval` with a `where` clause to filter your results.

```
... | where avg_bytes > 2 * moving_avg_bytes
```

And by looking at the table view or as an alert, you'll only see the times when the `avg_bytes` spiked.

To learn more about the trendline search command, see http://splunk.com/goto/book#trendline

---

Compacting Time-Based Charting

Problem

You would like to be able to visualize multiple trends in your data in a small space. This is the idea behind sparklines—small, time-based charts displayed within cells of your results table. Sparklines were invented by Edward Tufte and incorporated in Splunk 4.3.

Solution

To produce these sparklines in your tables, simply enclose your `stats` or `chart` functions in the `sparkline()` function.

Here, we'll use the example of web access logs. We want to create a small graph showing how long it took for each of our web pages to respond (assuming the field `spent` is the amount of time spent serving that web page). We have many pages, so we'll sort them to find the pages accessed the most (i.e., having the largest `count` values). The `5m` tells Splunk to show details down to a 5-minute granularity in the sparklines.

```
sourcetype=access*
| stats sparkline(avg(spent),5m), count by file
| sort - count
```

Run this search over the last hour. The result is a series of mini graphs showing how long it took each page to load on average, over time.

Variations

Try using different functions other than `avg`. Try using values different than `5m` for granularity. If you remove the `5m` granularity altogether, Splunk automatically picks the right value for the search timespan.

Reporting on Fields Inside XML or JSON

Problem

You need to report on data formatted in XML or JSON.

Solution

Use the `spath` command, introduced in Splunk 4.3, to extract values from XML- and JSON-formatted data. In this example, we'll assume a source type of book data in XML or JSON. We'll run a search that returns XML or JSON as the event's text, and use the `spath` command to extract the author name:

```
sourcetype=books
| spath output=author path=catalog.book.author
```

When called with no `path` argument, `spath` extracts all fields from the first 5000 characters, which is configurable, creating fields for each path element. Paths have the form `foo.bar.baz`. Each level can have an optional array index, indicated by curly braces (e.g., `foo{1}.bar`). All array elements can be represented by empty curly brackets (e.g., `foo{}`). The final level for XML queries can also include an attribute name, also enclosed by curly brackets (e.g., `foo.bar{@title}`) and prefaced with a `@`.

After you have the extracted field, you can report on it:

```
...  | top author
```

Variations

An older search command called `xmlkv` extracts simple XML key-value pairs. For example, calling `...  | xmlkv` on events that have a value of `<foo>bar</foo>` creates a field `foo` with a value bar. Another older command that extracts fields from XML is `xpath`.

Extracting Fields from an Event

Problem

You want to search for a pattern and extract that information from your events.

Solution

Using commands to extract fields is convenient for quickly extracting fields that are needed temporarily or that apply to specific searches and are not as general as a source or source type.

Regular Expressions

The `rex` command facilitates field extraction using regular expressions. For example, on email data, the following search extracts the from and to fields from email data using the `rex` command:

```
sourcetype=sendmail_syslog
| rex "From: (?<from>.*) To: (?<to>.*)"
```

Delimiters

If you're working with multiple fields that have delimiters around them, use the `extract` command to extract them.

Suppose your events look like this:

```
|height:72|age:43|name:matt smith|
```

Extract the `event` fields without delimiters using:

```
...  | extract pairdelim="|" kvdelim=":"
```

The result is what you would expect:

```
height=72, age=43, and name=matt smith.
```

Variations

Try using multikv, spath, or xmlkv.

Alerting Recipes

Recall from Chapter 5 that an alert is made up of two parts:

- A condition: An interesting thing you want to know about.

- An action: what to do when that interesting thing happens.

In addition, you can use throttling to prevent over-firing of repeated alerts of the same type.

For example:

- I want to get an email whenever one of my servers has a load above a certain percentage.

- I want to get an email of all servers whose load is above a certain percentage, but don't spam my inbox, so throttle the alerts for every 24 hours.

Alerting by Email when a Server Hits a Predefined Load

Problem

You want to be notified by email when a server load goes above 80%.

Solution

The following search retrieves events with load averages above 80% and calculates the maximum value for each host. The "top" source type comes with the Splunk Unix app (available at splunkbase.com), and is fed data from the Unix top command every 5 seconds:

```
sourcetype=top load_avg>80
| stats max(load_avg) by host
```

Set up the alert in the following way, using the instructions from Chapter 5:

- Alert condition: alert if the search returns at least one result.

- Alert actions: email and set subject to: Server load above 80%.

- Suppress: 1 hour.

Variations

Change alert conditions and suppression times

Alerting When Web Server Performance Slows

Problem

You want to be notified by email whenever the 95th percentile response time of your web servers is above a certain number of milliseconds.

Solution

The following search retrieves weblog events, calculates the 95th percentile response time for each unique web address (`uri_path`), and finally filters out any values where the 95th percentile is less than 200 milliseconds:

sourcetype=weblog

| stats perc95(response_time) AS resp_time_95 by uri_path

| where resp_time_95>200

Set up the alert in the following way:

- Alert condition: alert if the search returns at least X results (the number of slow web requests you think merit an alert being fired).

- Alert actions: email, with subject set to: "Web servers running slow." If you're running in the cloud (for example, on Amazon EC2™), maybe start new web server instances.

- Suppress: 1 hour.

Shutting Down Unneeded EC2 Instances

Problem

You want to shut down underutilized EC2 instances.

Solution

The following search retrieves weblog events and returns a table of hosts that have fewer than 10000 requests (over the timeframe that the search runs):

```
sourcetype=weblog
| stats count by host
| where count<10000
```

Set up the alert in the following way:

- Alert condition: alert if the search returns at least X results (the number of hosts you think merit an alert being fired).
- Alert actions: trigger a script that removes servers from the load balancer and shuts them down.
- Suppress: 10 minutes.

Converting Monitoring to Alerting

The monitoring recipes in this chapter produce useful reports, valuable in themselves. But, if you take a second look, many of these can also be the basis for setting up alerts, enabling Splunk to monitor the situation for you.

Here we'll briefly discuss converting a few of the monitoring recipes into alerts.

Monitoring Concurrent Users

This recipe can be made into an alert by using its search with a custom alert condition of "where max(concurrency) > 20". This alerts you if too many concurrent users are logged in.

Variations: Consider calculating the average concurrency as well and alerting if the max is twice the average.

Monitoring Inactive Hosts

A custom alert condition of where now() - recentTime > 60*60 alerts you if a host has not been heard from in over an hour.

Comparing Today's Top Values to Last Month's

A custom alert condition of where diff < -10 alerts you if an artist shoots to number 1 today and was not in the top 10 for the last month.

Variations: Use the same recipe to monitor HTTP status codes and report if a status code (e.g., 404) suddenly becomes significantly more, or less, prevalent than it was over the last month.

Find Metrics That Fell by 10% in an Hour

This recipe is already set up conveniently for an alert. Fire an alert when any events are seen.

Variation: Fire only when more than N declines are seen in a row.

Show a Moving Trendline and Identify Spikes

The variation for this recipe is already set up conveniently for an alert. Fire an alert when any events are seen.

Variations: Fire only when more than N spikes are seen in a time period (e.g., 5 minutes).

You might find it a useful exercise to add alerting to the remaining monitoring recipes.

7 Grouping Events

These recipes offer quick solutions to some of the most common, real-world problems we see that can be solved by grouping events.

Introduction

There are several ways to group events. The most common approach uses either the `transaction` or `stats` command. But when should you use `transaction` and when should you use `stats`?

The rule of thumb: If you can use `stats`, use `stats`. It's faster than `transaction`, especially in a distributed environment. With that speed, however, comes some limitations. You can only group events with `stats` if they have at least one common field value and if you require no other constraints. Typically, the raw event text is discarded.

Like `stats`, the `transaction` command can group events based on common field values, but it can also use more complex constraints such as total time span of the transaction, delays between events within the transaction, and required beginning and ending events. Unlike `stats`, `transaction` retains the raw event text and field values from the original events, but it does not compute any statistics over the grouped events, other than the `duration` (the delta of the `_time` field between oldest and newest events in the transaction) and the `eventcount` (the total number of events in the transaction).

The `transaction` command is most useful in two specific cases:

- When unique field values (also known as identifiers) are not sufficient to discriminate between discrete transactions. This is the case when an identifier might be reused, for example in web sessions identified by cookie/client IP. In this case, timespans or pauses should be used to segment the data into transactions. In other cases, when an identifier is reused, for example in DHCP logs, a particular message may identify the beginning or end of a transaction.

- When it is desirable to see the raw text of the events rather than an analysis on the constituent fields of the events.

Again, when neither of these cases is applicable, it is a better practice to use `stats`, as search performance for `stats` is generally better than `transaction`. Often there is a unique identifier, and `stats` can be used.

For example, to compute statistics on the duration of trades identified by the unique identifier `trade_id`, the following searches yield the same answer:

```
… | transaction trade_id
  | chart count by duration
… | stats range(_time) as duration by trade_id
  | chart count by duration
```

The second search is more efficient.

However, if `trade_id` values are reused but the last event of each trade is indicated by the text "END", the only viable solution is:

```
… | transaction trade_id endswith=END
  | chart count by duration
```

If, instead of an end condition, `trade_id` values are not reused within 10 minutes, the most viable solution is:

```
… | transaction trade_id maxpause=10m
  | chart count by duration
```

Finally, a brief word about performance. No matter what search commands you use, it's imperative for performance that you make the base search as specific as possible. Consider this search:

```
sourcetype=x | transaction field=ip maxpause=15s | search
ip=1.2.3.4
```

Here we are retrieving all events of `sourcetype=x`, building up transactions, and then throwing away any that don't have an `ip=1.2.3.4`. If all your events have the same `ip` value, this search should be:

```
sourcetype=x ip=1.2.3.4 | transaction field=ip maxpause=15s
```

This search retrieves only the events it needs to and is much more efficient. More about this is in "Finding Specific Transactions" later in this chapter.

Recipes

Unifying Field Names

Problem

You need to build transactions from multiple data sources that use different field names for the same identifier.

Solution

Typically, you can join transactions with common fields like:

```
... | transaction username
```

But when the `username` identifier is called different names (login, name, user, owner, and so on) in different data sources, you need to normalize the field names.

If sourcetype `A` only contains `field_A` and sourcetype `B` only contains `field_B`, create a new field called `field_Z` which is either `field_A` or `field_B`, depending on which is present in an event. You can then build the transaction based on the value of `field_Z`.

```
sourcetype=A OR sourcetype=B
| eval field_Z = coalesce(field_A, field_B)
| transaction field_Z
```

Variations

Above we invoked `coalesce` to use whichever field was present on an event, but sometimes you will need to use some logic to decide which field to use in unifying events. `eval`'s `if` or `case` functions may come in handy.

Finding Incomplete Transactions

Problem

You need to report on incomplete transactions, such as users who have logged in but not logged out.

Solution

Suppose you are searching for user sessions starting with a login and ending with a logout:

```
… | transaction userid startswith="login"
    endswith="logout"
```

You would like to build a report that shows incomplete transactions—users who have logged in but not logged out. How can you achieve this?

The `transaction` command creates an internal boolean field named `closed_txn` to indicate if a given transaction is complete or not. Normally incomplete transactions are not returned, but you can ask for these "evicted" partial transactions by specifying the parameter `keepevicted=true`. Evicted transactions are sets of events that do not match all the transaction parameters. For example, the time requirements are not met in an evicted transaction. Transactions that fulfill all the requirements are marked as complete by having the field `closed_txn` set to 1 (rather than 0 for incomplete transactions). So the pattern for finding incomplete transactions would generally be:

```
… | transaction <conditions> keepevicted=true
  | search closed_txn=0
```

In our case, however, there's a wrinkle. An `endswith` condition *not* matching will not set the `closed_txn=0` because events are processed from newest to oldest. Technically, the `endswith` condition starts the transaction, in terms of processing. To get around this, we need to filter transactions based on the `closed_txn` field, as well as make sure that our transactions don't have both a `login` and a `logout`:

```
… | transaction userid  startswith="login"
                        endswith="logout"
  keepevicted=true
  | search closed_txn=0 NOT (login logout)
```

Variations

A variation on this solution is to use `stats`, if your transactions don't have `startswith`/`endswith` conditions or time constraints, and you don't care about preserving the actual `transaction`. In this example, you just want the `userid` of users who haven't logged out.

First, we can search specifically for login and logout events:

```
action="login" OR action="logout"
```

Next, for each `userid`, we use `stats` to keep track of the `action` seen per `userid`. Because events are in time descending order, the first action is the most recent.

> ... | stats first(action) as last_action by userid

Finally, we keep only events where the most recent user action was a login:

> ... | search last_action="login"

At this point we have the list of all `userid` values where the last action was a login.

Calculating Times within Transactions

Problem

You need to find the duration times between events in a transaction.

Solution

The basic approach is to use the `eval` command to mark the points in time needed to measure the different durations, and then calculate the durations between these points using `eval` after the `transaction` command.

Note: *In this chapter, sample events in a transaction are numbered so that we can refer to them as event1, event2, and so on.*

For example, suppose you have a transaction made up of four events, unified by a common `id` field and you want to measure the duration of phase1 and phase2:

> [1] Tue Jul 6 09:16:00 id=1234 start of event.
> [2] Tue Jul 6 09:16:10 id=1234 phase1: do some work.
> [3] Tue Jul 6 09:16:40 id=1234 phase2: do some more.
> [4] Tue Jul 6 09:17:00 id=1234 end of event.

By default, the timestamp of this transaction-based event will be from the first event (event1), and the duration will be the difference in time between event4 and event1.

To get the duration of phase1, we'll need to mark timestamps for event2 and event3. `eval`'s `searchmatch` function works well for this example, but you have the full range of `eval` functions available to you for more complex situations.

```
...| eval p1start = if(searchmatch("phase1"), _time, null())
   | eval p2start = if(searchmatch("phase2"), _time, null())
```

Next we make the actual transactions:

```
... | transaction id startswith="start of event"
                      endswith="end of event"
```

Finally we calculate the duration for each `transaction`, using the values calculated above.

```
...| eval p1_duration = p2start - p1start
   | eval p2_duration = (_time + duration) - p2start
```

In this example, we calculated the time of the last event by added `_time` (the time of the first event) and adding duration to it. Once we knew the last event's time, we calculated `p2_duration` as the difference between the last event and the start of phase2.

Variations

By default, the `transaction` command makes multivalued fields out of the field values seen in more than one of a transaction's composite events, but those values are just kept as an unordered, deduplicated bag of values. For example, if a transaction is made of 4 events, and those events each have a name field as follows—name=matt, name=amy, name=rory, name=amy—then the transaction made up of four events will have a multivalued field name with values of "amy", "matt", and "rory". Note that we've lost the order in which the events occurred and we've missed an "amy"! To keep the entire list of values, in order, use the `mvlist` option.

Here, we're building a transaction and keeping the list of times for its events:

```
... | eval times=_time | transaction id mvlist="times"
```

From here we can add on `eval` commands to calculate differences. We can calculate the time between the first and second event in the transaction as follows:

```
... | eval diff_1_2 = mvindex(times,1) - mvindex(times,0)
```

Finding the Latest Events

Problem

You need to find the latest event for each unique field value. For example, when was the last time each user logged in?

Solution

At first, you might be tempted to use the `transaction` or `stats` command. For example, this search returns, for each unique `userid`, the first value seen for each field:

```
… | stats first(*) by userid
```

Note that this search returns the first value of each field seen for events that have the same `userid`. It provides a union of all events that have that user ID, which is not what we want. What we want is the first event with a unique `userid`. The proper way to do that is with the `dedup` command:

```
… | dedup userid
```

Variations

If you want to get the oldest (not the newest) event with a unique `userid`, use the `sortby` clause of the `dedup` command:

```
… | dedup userid sortby + _time
```

Finding Repeated Events

Problem

You want to group all events with repeated occurrences of a value in order to remove noise from reports and alerts.

Solution

Suppose you have events as follows:

```
2012-07-22 11:45:23 code=239
2012-07-22 11:45:25 code=773
2012-07-22 11:45:26 code=-1
2012-07-22 11:45:27 code=-1
2012-07-22 11:45:28 code=-1
2012-07-22 11:45:29 code=292
2012-07-22 11:45:30 code=292
2012-07-22 11:45:32 code=-1
2012-07-22 11:45:33 code=444
2012-07-22 11:45:35 code=-1
2012-07-22 11:45:36 code=-1
```

Your goal is to get 7 events, one for each of the code values in a row: 239, 773, -1, 292, -1, 444, -1. You might be tempted to use the `transaction` command as follows:

```
… | transaction code
```

Using `transaction` here is a case of applying the wrong tool for the job. As long as we don't really care about the number of repeated runs of duplicates, the more straightforward approach is to use `dedup`, which removes duplicates. By default, `dedup` will remove all duplicate events (where an event is a duplicate if it has the same values for the specified fields). But that's not what we want; we want to remove duplicates that appear in a cluster. To do this, `dedup` has a `consecutive=true` option that tells it to remove only duplicates that are consecutive.

```
... | dedup code consecutive=true
```

Time Between Transactions

Problem

You want to determine the time between transactions, such as how long it's been between user visits to your website.

Solution

Suppose we have a basic `transaction` search that groups all events by a given user (`clientip-cookie` pair), but splits the transactions when the user is inactive for 10 minutes:

```
... | transaction clientip, cookie maxpause=10m
```

Ultimately, our goal is to calculate, for each `clientip-cookie` pair, the difference in time between the end time of a transaction and the start time of a more recent (i.e. 'previous' in order of events returned) transaction. That time difference is the gap between transactions. For example, suppose we had two pseudo transactions, returned from most recent to oldest:

```
T1: start=10:30 end=10:40 clientip=a cookie=x
T2: start=10:10 end=10:20 clientip=a cookie=x
```

The gap in time between these two transactions is the difference between the start time of T1 (10:30) and the end time of T2 (10:20), or 10 minutes. The rest of this recipe explains how to calculate these values.

First, we need to calculate the end time of each transaction, keeping in mind that the timestamp of a transaction is the time that the first event occurred and the duration is the number of seconds that elapsed between the first and last event in the transaction:

```
... | eval end_time = _time + duration
```

Next we need to add the start time from the previous (i.e., more recent) transaction to each transaction. That will allow us to calculate the difference between the start time of the previous transaction and our calculated `end_time`.

To do this we can use `streamstats` to calculate the last value of the start time (`_time`) seen in a sliding window of just one transaction—`global=false` and `window=1`—and to ignore the current event in that sliding window—`current=false`. In effect, we're instructing `streamstats` to look only at the previous event's value. Finally, note that we're specifying that this window is only applicable to the given user (`clientip-cookie` pair):

```
... | streamstats first(_time) as prev_starttime
global=false window=1 current=false
by clientip, cookie
```

At this point, the relevant fields might look something like this:

```
T1: _time=10:00:06, duration=4, end_time=10:00:10
T2: _time=10:00:01, duration=2, end_time=10:00:03
   prev_starttime=10:00:06
T3: _time=10:00:00, duration=0, end_time=10:00:01
   prev_starttime=10:00:01
```

Now, we can finally calculate the difference in time between the previous transaction's start time (`prev_starttime`) and the calculated `end_time`. That difference is the gap between transactions, the amount of time (in seconds) passed between two consecutive transactions from the same user (`clientip-cookie` pair).

```
... | eval gap_time = prev_starttime - end_time
```

Putting it all together, the search becomes:

```
... | transaction clientip, cookie maxpause=10m
   | eval end_time = _time + duration
   | streamstats first(_time) as prev_starttime
global=false window=1 current=false
by clientip, cookie
   | eval gap_time = prev_starttime - end_time
```

At this point you can do report on `gap_time` values. For example, what is the biggest and average gap length per user?

```
... | stats max(gap_time) as max,
            avg(gap_time) as avg
            by clientip, cookie
```

Variations

Given a simpler set of requirements, we can calculate the gaps between events in a much simpler way. If the only constraints for transactions are `startswith` and `endswith`—meaning there are no time (e.g., `maxpause=10m`) or field (e.g., `clientip`, `cookie`) constraints— then we can calculate the gaps in transactions by simply swapping the `startswith` and `endswith` values.

For example, given these events:

```
10:00:01 login
10:00:02 logout
10:00:08 login
10:00:10 logout
10:00:15 login
10:00:16 logout
```

Rather than:

```
… | transaction startswith="login" endswith="logout"
```

We can make the *gaps* between the standard transactions (login then logout) be the transactions instead (logout then login):

```
… | transaction endswith="login" startswith="logout"
```

From here the transactions are the gaps between logout and login events, so we can subsequently calculate gap statistics using `duration`:

```
… | stats max(duration) as max, avg(duration) as avg
```

Another variation on the theme of finding time between events is if you are interested in the time between a given event (event A) and the most proximate newer event (event B). By using `streamstats`, you can determine the range of times between the last two events, which is the difference between the current event and the previous event:

```
… | streamstats range(_time) as duration window=2
```

Finding Specific Transactions

Problem

You need to find transactions with specific field values.

Solution

A general search for all transactions might look like this:

```
sourcetype=email_logs | transaction userid
```

Suppose, however, that we want to identify just those transactions where there is an event that has the field/value pairs `to=root` and `from=msmith`. You could use this search:

```
sourcetype=email_logs
| transaction userid
| search to=root from=msmith
```

The problem here is that you are retrieving all events from this sourcetype (potentially billions), building up all the transactions, and then throwing 99% of the data right in to the bit bucket. Not only is it slow, but it is also painfully inefficient.

You might be tempted to reduce the data coming in as follows:

```
sourcetype=email_logs (to=root OR from=msmith)
| transaction userid
| search to=root from=msmith
```

Although you are not inefficiently retrieving all the events from the given sourcetype, there are two additional problems. The first problem is fatal: you are getting only a fraction of the events needed to solve your problem. Specifically, you are only retrieving events that have a `to` or a `from` field. Using this syntax, you are missing all the other events that could make up the transaction. For example, suppose this is what the full transaction should look like:

```
[1] 10/15/2012 10:11:12 userid=123 to=root
[2] 10/15/2012 10:11:13 userid=123 from=msmith
[3] 10/15/2012 10:11:14 userid=123 subject="serious error"
[4] 10/15/2012 10:11:15 userid=123 server=mailserver
[5] 10/15/2012 10:11:16 userid=123 priority=high
```

The above search will not get event3, which has `subject`, or event4, which has `server`, and it will not be possible for Splunk to return the complete transaction.

The second problem with the search is that `to=root` might be very common and you could actually be retrieving too many events and building too many transactions.

So what is the solution? There are two methods: using subsearches and using the `searchtxn` command.

Using Subsearches

Your goal is to get all the `userid` values for events that have `to=root`, or `from=msmith`. Pick the more rare condition to get the candidate `userid` values as quickly as possible. Let's assume that `from=msmith` is more rare:

```
sourcetype=email_logs from=msmith
| dedup userid
| fields userid
```

Now that you have the relevant `userid` values, you can search for just those events that contain these values and more efficiently build the transaction:

```
... | transaction userid
```

Finally, filter the transactions to make sure that they have `to=root` and `from=msmith` (it's possible that a `userid` value is used for other `to` and `from` values):

```
... | search to=root AND from=msmith
```

Putting this all together, with the first search as a subsearch passing the userid to the outer search:

```
[
search sourcetype=email_logs from=msmith
| dedup userid
| fields userid
]
| transaction userid
| search to=root from=msmith
```

Use searchtxn

The `searchtxn` ("search transaction") command does the subsearch legwork for you. It searches for just the events needed to build a `transaction`. Specifically, `searchtxn` does transitive closure of fields needed for `transaction`, running the searches needed to find events for transaction, then running the `transaction` search, and finally filtering them to the specified constraints. If you were unifying your events by more than one field, the subsearch solution becomes tricky. `searchtxn` also determines which seed condition is rarer to get the fastest results. Thus, your search for email transactions with `to=root` and `from=msmith`, simply becomes:

```
| searchtxn email_txn to=root from=msmith
```

But what is `email_txn` in the above search? It refers to a transaction-type definition that has to be created in a Splunk config file—`transaction-type.conf`. In this case, `transactiontype.conf` might look like:

```
[email_txn]
fields=userid
search = sourcetype=email_logs
```

Running the `searchtxn` search will automatically run the search:

```
sourcetype=email_logs from=msmith | dedup userid
```

The result of that search gives `searchtxn` the list of the `userids` to operate upon. It then runs another search for:

```
sourcetype=email_logs (userid=123 OR userid=369 OR use-
rid=576 ...)
| transaction name=email_txn
| search to=root from=msmith
```

This search returns the needle-in-the-haystack transactions from the results returned by the `searchtxn` search.

Note: If the `transaction` command's field list had more than one field, `searchtxn` would automatically run multiple searches to get a transitive closure of all values needed.

Variations

Explore using multiple fields with the `searchtxn` command. If you're interested in getting the relevant events and don't want `searchtxn` to actually build the transactions, use `eventsonly=true`.

Finding Events Near Other Events

Problem

You need to find events before and after another event. Suppose you want to search for logins by root and then search backwards up to a minute for unsuccessful root logins as well as forward up to a minute for changes in passwords.

Solution

One solution is to use subsearches and look for the last instance of this scenario. Do a subsearch for root logins and return `starttimeu` and `end-timeu`, which then scopes the parent search to those time boundaries when searching for either a `failed_login` or a `password_changed` from the same `src_ip`:

```
[
search sourcetype=login_data action=login user=root
| eval starttimeu=_time - 60
| eval endtimeu=_time + 60
| return starttimeu, endtimeu, src_ip
]
action=failed_login OR action=password_changed
```

The downside to this approach is that it only finds the last instance of a login and possibly has false positives, as it doesn't distinguish between `failed_logins` afterward or `password_changed` before.

Instead, the problem can be solved by filtering the events down to just those we care about:

```
sourcetype=login_data ( action=login OR action=failed_login
OR action=password_changed )
```

The transaction should consist of events from the same `src_ip` that start with a `failed_login` and end with a `password_changed`. Furthermore, the transaction should span no more than 2 minutes from start to finish:

```
... | transaction src_ip maxspan=2m
           startswith=(action=failed_login)
           endswith=(action=password_changed)
```

Finally, you need to filter for only those transactions that have `user=root`. Since a `failed_login` event often won't have `user=root` (the user hasn't logged in), it is necessary to filter after the transaction:

```
... | search user=root
```

Conversely, if it was certain that `user=root` was in all the relevant events, it should be added to the search clause, skipping the final filtering (`search user=root`).

Finding Events After Events

Problem

You need to get the first 3 events after a particular event (for example, a login event) but there is no well-defined ending event.

Solution

Given the following ideal transaction that starts with a login action:

```
[1] 10:11:12 src_ip=10.0.0.5 user=root action=login
[2] 10:11:13 src_ip=10.0.0.5 user=root action="cd /"
[3] 10:11:14 src_ip=10.0.0.5 user=root action="rm -rf *"
[4] 10:11:15 src_ip=10.0.0.5 user=root server="echo lol"
```

The obvious search choice is to use `transaction` that `startswith` the login action:

```
... | transaction src_ip, user startswith="(action=login)"
maxevents=4
```

The problem is that you will get transactions that don't have `action=login`. Why? The `startswith` option does not tell `transaction` to return only transactions that actually begin with the string you're supplying. Rather it tells `transaction` that when it encounters a line that matches the `startswith` directive, it is the beginning of a new transaction. However, transactions will also be made for different values of `src_ip`, regardless of the `startswith` condition.

To avoid this, add a filtering search command after the `transaction` search above:

```
... | search action=login
```

The transactions returned will start with `action=login` and include the next three events for the `src_ip` and `user`.

Note: *If there are less than three events between two logins, the transaction will be smaller than 4 events. The* transaction *command adds an* eventcount *field to each transaction, which you can then use to further filter transactions.*

Grouping Groups

Problem

You need to build transactions with multiple fields that change value within the transaction.

Solution

Suppose you want to build a transaction from these four events, unified by the host and cookie fields:

```
[1] host=a
[2] host=a cookie=b
[3] host=b
[4] host=b cookie=b
```

Because the value of host changes during this transaction, a simple transaction command unfortunately will make two distinct transactions:

```
... | transaction host, cookie
```

When it sees event1 and event2, it builds a transaction with host=a, but when it gets to event3, which has a different value for host (host=b), it puts event3 and event4 into a separate transaction of events that have host=b. The result is that these four events are turned into two transactions, rather than one transaction based on the common value of cookie:

Transaction1:

```
[1] host=a
[2] host=a cookie=b
```

Transaction2:

```
[3] host=b
[4] host=b cookie=b
```

You might be tempted to remove the host field from the transaction command and unify the transactions based on the cookie value. The problem is that this would create a transaction with event2 and event4, ignoring event1 and event3 because they do not have a cookie value.

The solution to this problem is to build a transaction on top of a transaction:

```
... | transaction host, cookie | transaction cookie
```

This second transaction command will take the above two transactions and unify them with a common cookie field.

Note that if you care about the calculated fields duration and event-count, they are now incorrect. The duration after the second transaction command will be the difference between the transactions it unifies rather than the events that comprise it. Similarly, the eventcount will be the number of transactions it unified, rather that the correct number of events.

To get the correct eventcount after the first transaction command, create a field called mycount to store all the eventcount values, and then after the second `transaction` command sum all the `mycount` values to calculate the `real_eventcount`. Similarly, after the first `transaction` command, record the start and end times of each transaction and then after the second `transaction` command get the minimum start time and the maximum end time to calculate the `real_duration`:

```
... | transaction host, cookie
| eval mycount=eventcount
| eval mystart=_time
| eval myend=duration + _time
| transaction cookie mvlist="mycount"
| eval first = min(mystart)
| eval last=max(myend)
| eval real_duration=last-first
| eval real_eventcount = sum(mycount)
```

8   Lookup Tables

These lookup table recipes briefly show advanced solutions to common, real-world problems. Splunk's lookup feature lets you reference fields in an external CSV file that match fields in your event data. Using this match, you can enrich your event data with additional fields. Note that we do not cover external scripted lookups or time-based lookups.

Introduction

These recipes extensively use three lookup search commands: `lookup`, `inputlookup`, and `outputlookup`.

lookup

For each event, this command finds matching rows in an external CSV table and returns the other column values, enriching the events. For example, an event with a `host` field value and a lookup table that has `host` and `machine_type` rows, specifying `… | lookup mylookup host` adds the `machine_type` value corresponding to the `host` value to each event. By default, matching is case-sensitive and does not support wildcards, but you can configure these options. Using the `lookup` command matches values in external tables explicitly. Automatic lookups, which are set up using Splunk Manager, match values implicitly. To learn more about configuring automatic lookups, see http://splunk.com/goto/book#autolookup.

inputlookup

This command returns the whole lookup table as search results. For example, `… | inputlookup mylookup` returns a search result for each row in the table `mylookup`, which has two field values: `host` and `machine_type`.

outputlookup

You might wonder how to create a lookup table. This command outputs the current search results to a lookup table on disk. For example, `… | outputlookup mytable.csv` saves all the results into `mytable.csv`.

Further Reading

http://splunk.com/goto/book#lookuptutorial

http://splunk.com/goto/book#externallookups

Recipes

Setting Default Lookup Values

Problem

You need a default field value if an event's value is not in the lookup table.

Solution

There are several solutions.

Using an explicit `lookup`, you can simply use the `eval coalesce` function:

```
… | lookup mylookup ip | eval domain=coalesce(domain,"unkno
wn")
```

Using automatic lookups, there's a setting for that. Go to **Manager >> Lookups >> Lookup Definition >> mylookup**, select the **Advanced options** checkbox, and make the following changes:

Set **Minimum matches**: 1

Set **Default matches**: unknown

Save the changes.

Using Reverse Lookups

Problem

You need to search for events based on the output of a lookup table.

Solution

Splunk permits you to use reverse lookup searches, meaning you can search for the output value of an automatic lookup and Splunk can translate that into a search for the corresponding input fields of the lookup.

For example, suppose you have a lookup table mapping machine_name to owner:

```
machine_name, owner
webserver1,erik
dbserver7,stephen
dbserver8,amrit
...
```

If your events have a machine_name field and if you wanted to search for a particular owner, erik, you might use an expensive search, like this:

```
... | lookup mylookup machine_name | search owner=erik
```

This search is expensive because you're retrieving all of your events and filtering out any that don't have erik as the owner.

Alternatively, you might consider an efficient but complicated subsearch:

```
... [ inputlookup mylookup | search owner=erik | fields machine_name]
```

This search retrieves all the rows of the lookup table, filters out any rows that don't have erik as the owner, and returns a big OR expression of machine names for Splunk to ultimately run a search on.

But none of this is necessary. If you've set up an automatic lookup table, you can simply ask Splunk to search for owner=erik.

That's it. Effectively, Splunk does the subsearch solution behind the scenes, generating the search of OR clauses for you.

Note: *Splunk also does automatic reverse searching for defined field extraction, tags, and eventtypes—you can search for the value that would be extracted, tagged, or typed, and Splunk retrieves the correct events.*

Variations

Using automatic lookups and the built-in reverse lookups, you can recreate Splunk's tagging system. For example, make a mapping from host to your field called host_tag. Now you can search for events based on their host_tag and not only the host value. Many people find it easier to maintain lookup tables than the Splunk tags.

Using a Two-Tiered Lookup

Problem

You need to do a two-layered lookup. For example, look up an IP address in a table of common, well-known hosts and, if that fails for a given event, then and only then use a secondary, more expensive full DNS lookup.

Solution

After we've retrieved events, we do our initial lookup against local_dns. csv, a local lookup file:

```
...  | lookup local_dns ip OUTPUT hostname
```

If the lookup doesn't match, the `hostname` field is null for that event.

We now perform the second, expensive lookup on events that have no `hostname`. By using `OUTPUTNEW` instead of `OUTPUT`, the lookup will only run on events that have a null value for `hostname`.

```
...  | lookup dnslookup ip OUTPUTNEW hostname
```

Putting it all together:

```
...  | lookup local_dns ip OUTPUT hostname
     | lookup dnslookup ip OUTPUTNEW hostname
```

Using Multistep Lookups

Problem

You need to look up a value in one lookup file and use a returned field value from that first lookup to do a second lookup using a different lookup file.

Solution

You can do this manually by running sequential lookup commands. For example, if a first lookup table takes values of field A and outputs values of field B, and a second lookup table takes values of field B and outputs values of field C:

```
...  | lookup my_first_lookup A | lookup my_second_lookup B
```

More interestingly, this can be done using automatic lookups, where this chaining happens automatically. It is imperative, however, that the lookups are run in the correct order, by using the alphanumeric precedence of property names.

Go to **Manager >> Lookups >> Automatic lookups**, and create two automatic lookups, making sure that the one to run later has a named value greater than the previous lookup name. For example:

```
0_first_lookup = my_first_lookup A OUTPUT B
1_second_lookup = my_second_lookup B OUTPUT C
```

Note: *Using lookup chaining as shown in this recipe, reverse lookups as in the "Using Reverse Lookups" recipe do not work because Splunk is currently not able to reverse multiple steps of automatic field lookups (e.g., automatically converting a search for chained output field value* C=baz *into a search for input field value* A=foo*).*

Creating a Lookup Table from Search Results

Problem

You want to create a lookup table from search results.

Solution

If you were to simply do:

```
<some search> | outputlookup mylookupfile.csv
```

you might encounter two problems. First, events have many fields, including internal fields like _raw, and _time, which you don't want in your lookup table. Second, of the fields you do care about, most likely there are duplicate values on the events retrieved. To handle the first problem, we won't use the `fields` command because it's inconvenient to remove internal fields. Instead, we'll use the `table` command to better limit the fields to what we explicitly specify. To solve the second problem, use the `dedup` command. Putting it all together:

```
… | table field1, field2
   | dedup field1
   | outputlookup mylookupfile.csv
```

Appending Results to Lookup Tables

Problem

You need to append results to an existing lookup table. For example, you want to create a single lookup table based on the results of multiple iterations of the same search. Specifically, suppose you wanted to keep track of the last IP each user logged in from. You might want to run a job every 15 minutes to look that up and update the lookup table with new users.

Solution

The basic procedure is to get the set of results you want to append to the lookup table, use `inputlookup` to append the current contents of the lookup, and use `outputlookup` to write the lookup. The command looks like this:

```
your_search_to_retrieve_values_needed
| fields the_interesting_fields
| inputlookup mylookup append=true
| dedup the_interesting_fields
| outputlookup mylookup
```

First, we told Splunk to retrieve the new data and retain only the fields needed for the lookup table. Next, we used `inputlookup` to append the existing rows in `mylookup`, by using the `append=true` option. Next we remove duplicates with `dedup`. Finally, we used `outputlookup` to output all these results to `mylookup`.

Variations

Suppose you want your lookup table to have only the most recent 30 days of values. You can set up a lookup table to be updated daily from a scheduled search. When you set up your scheduled search to output the lookup table and before the `outputlookup` command, add a condition that filters out data older than 30 days:

```
... | where _time >= now() - (60*60*24*30)
```

where 60*60*60*24*30 is the number of seconds in 30 days.

Building on the previous example, our search becomes:

```
your_search_to_retrieve_values_needed
| fields just_the_interesting_fields
| inputlookup mylookup append=true
| where _time >= now() - (60*60*24*30)
| outputlookup mylookup
```

Obviously, you'll also need to keep `_time` as one of the fields in your lookup table.

Using Massive Lookup Tables

Problem

You have a massive lookup table but want performance to be fast.

Solution

When you have very large lookup tables and notice that performance is affected, there are several solutions.

First, consider whether you can make smaller, more specific lookup tables. For example, if some of your searches need only a subset of the rows and columns, consider making a concise version of the lookup for those searches. The following search reduced the size of `mylookup` table by reducing the rows to those that meet some condition, removing duplicates, removing all columns but a needed input and output field, and finally writing the results to the `mylookup2` table.

```
| inputlookup mylookup
| search somecondition
| dedup someinputfield
| table someinputfield, someoutputfield
| outputlookup mylookup2
```

If you can't reduce the size of the lookup table, there are other solutions. If your Splunk installation has several indexers, those indexers automatically replicate your lookup table. But if the lookup file is very large (e.g., 100MB), this may take a very long time long.

One solution, if your bundles are being frequently updated, is to disable bundle replication and instead use NFS to make the bundles available to all nodes.

See: http://splunk.com/goto/book#mount

Another solution, if your lookup table doesn't change too often and you cannot rely on shared and mounted drives, is to use local lookups.

- To prevent the lookup from being replicated and distributed, add the lookup table to the `replicationBlacklist` in `distsearch.conf`. (See http://splunk.com/goto/book#distributed)

- Copy the lookup table CSV file to each of your indexers in `$SPLUNK_HOME/etc/system/lookup`

- When you run the search, add `local=true` option to the `lookup` search command.

Note: *Lookup definitions defined to implicitly run via props.conf by their very nature are not local and must be distributed to indexers.*

Finally, consider moving away from large CSV files and consider using external lookups (usually leveraging a script that queries a database).

Note: *When a .csv lookup table reaches a certain size (10 MB by default), Splunk indexes it for faster access. By indexing the .csv file, Splunk can search rather than scan the table. To edit the size before a file is indexed, edit* `limits.conf`'s *lookup stanza and change the* `max_memtable_bytes` *value.*

Comparing Results to Lookup Values

Problem

You want to compare the values in the lookup list with those in your events. For example, you have a lookup table with IP addresses and want to know which IP addresses occur in your data.

Solution

If events with particular field values are a small subset of your events, you can efficiently use subsearches to find relevant events. Use `inputlookup` in a subsearch to generate a large OR search of all the values seen in your lookup table. The size of the list returned from a subsearch can be 10,000 items in size (modifiable in limits.conf).

```
yoursearch [ inputlookup mylookup | fields ip ]
```

The resulting search executed looks similar to:

```
yoursearch AND ( ip=1.2.3.4 OR ip=1.2.3.5 OR ... )
```

You can test what the subsearch returns by running the search that is inside the subsearch and appending the `format` command:

```
| inputlookup mylookup | fields ip | format
```

See: http://splunk.com/goto/book#subsearch

Variation I

Similarly, to retrieve events with values NOT in your lookup table, use a pattern like:

```
yoursearch NOT [ inputlookup mylookup | fields ip ]
```

which results in a search running like this:

```
yoursearch AND NOT ( ip=1.2.3.4 OR ip=1.2.3.5 OR ... )
```

Variation II

Alternatively, if you want values in your lookup table that are not matched in your data, use:

```
| inputlookup mylookup
| fields ip
| search NOT [ search yoursearch | dedup ip | fields ip ]
```

which takes all values in the lookup and filters out those that match your data.

Variation III

For massive lists, here is a tricky and efficient search pattern to find all the values in your events that are also in the lookup table: retrieve your events and then append the entire lookup table to the events. By setting a field (e.g., `marker`), we can keep track of whether a result (think 'row') is an event or a lookup table row. We can use `stats` to get the list of IP addresses that are in both lists (count>1):

```
yoursearch
| eval marker=data
| append [ inputlookup mylookup | eval marker=lookup ]
| stats dc(marker) as list_count by ip
| where list_count > 1
```

Note: *Although the append command appears to be executing a subsearch, it is not. There is no limit on the number of results appended, unlike a subsearch, which has a default limit of 10k results.*

If you need to use this technique over a very large timespan, it is more efficient to use another lookup table to maintain long-term state. In short, schedule a search over a shorter time window—such as one day—that calculates the last time an IP was seen. Then, use a combination of `inputlookup`, `dedup`, and `outputlookup` to incrementally update that lookup table over the very long haul. This gives you a very quick resource to look at to know the most recent state. See the "Appending Results to Lookup Tables" recipe for specifics.

Controlling Lookup Matches

Problem

You have multiple entries in a lookup table for a given combination of input fields and want the first value to match. For example, your lookup table maps hostnames to several host aliases, and you want the first alias.

Solution

By default, Splunk returns up to 100 matches for lookups not involving a time element. You can update it to return only one.

Using the UI, go to **Manager >> Lookups >> Lookup definitions** and edit or create your lookup definition. Select the **Advanced options** checkbox and enter **1** for **Maximum matches**.

Alternatively, you can edit the applicable `transforms.conf`. Add `max_matches=1` to your lookups stanza.

See: http://splunk.com/goto/book#field_lookup

Variations

If your lookup table has duplicates that you want to remove, you can clean them with a search similar to:

```
| inputlookup mylookup | dedup host | outputlookup mylookup
```

This eliminates all but the first distinct occurrence of each host in the file.

Matching IPs

Problem

You have a lookup table with ranges of IP addresses that you want to match.

Solution

Suppose your events have IP addresses in them and you have a table of IP ranges and ISPs:

```
network_range, isp
220.165.96.0/19, isp_name1
220.64.192.0/19, isp_name2

. . .
```

You can specify a `match_type` for a lookup. Unfortunately, this functionality isn't available in the UI but you can set it in the `transforms.conf` config file.

Set the `match_type` to `CIDR` for your `network_range`.

In `transforms.conf`:

```
[mylookup]
match_type = CIDR(network_range)
```

See: http://splunk.com/goto/book#transform

Variations

The available `match_type` values are `WILDCARD`, `CIDR`, and `EXACT`. `EXACT` is the default and does not need to be specified.

Also in `transforms.conf`, you can specify whether lookup matching should be case sensitive (the default) or not. To have matching be case insensitive, use:

```
case_sensitive_match = False
```

Matching with Wildcards

Problem

You need wildcard matching for your lookup table.

Solution

Suppose you have a lookup table with URLs you'd like to match on:

```
url, allowed
*.google.com/*, True
www.blacklist.org*, False
*/img/*jpg, False
```

By including wildcard (*) characters in your lookup table values, you can direct Splunk to match on wildcards.

As in the "Matching IPs" recipe, you can specify a `match_type` for a lookup in the `transforms.conf` config file:

```
[mylookup]
match_type = WILDCARD(url)
```

Note: *By default the maximum matches for lookup tables is 100, so if you have multiple rows that match, the output fields will have multiple values. For example, a url of "*www.google.com/img/pix.jpg*" would match the first and third row in the table above, and the allowed field would become a multivalued field with the values True and False. Usually this is not what you want. By setting the* **Maximum matches** *setting to 1, the first matching value will be used, and you case use the order of the table to determine precedence. You can find this setting at* **Manager >> Lookups >> Lookup Definition >> mylookup***, after selecting the* **Advanced options** *checkbox.*

Variations

This chapter's first recipe dealt with default values when a lookup fails to match. Yet another way to accomplish this is with wildcard matching. Make the last item in your lookup table have a match value of *, and set the minimum and maximum matches for your lookup table to be 1.

Appendix A: Machine Data Basics

Machine-generated data has long been used in the data center by IT professionals but has only recently been recognized as a new source for helping other departments. Sometimes called IT data or operational data, machine data is all of the data generated by applications, servers, network devices, security devices, and other systems in your business. The universe covered by machine data is much more than log files—it includes data from configuration, clickstreams, change events, diagnostics, APIs, message queues, and custom applications. This data is rigidly structured, time-series based, and high-volume. It's generated by almost every component in IT, and its formats and sources vary widely. Thousands of distinct log formats, many from custom applications, are critical to diagnosing service problems, detecting sophisticated security threats, and demonstrating compliance. And with the explosion of connected devices, the sheer amount of information being created by machines of all kinds—GPS devices, RFID tags, mobile phones, utility equipment, and so on—is expanding more quickly than our ability to process and use it.

The value of machine data is not news to IT professionals; they have used it for years. Increasingly, users of Splunk find that it can also help shed light on business issues. Machine data is most often stored in large files, and before Splunk, it would lie around dormant until problems arose and these files had to be manually inspected. With Splunk these files are indexed and useable.

Business users are used to dealing with data generated by people participating in business processes. Most often this transactional data, as it's called, is stored in one of two forms.

Relational databases are widely used to store transactional data. They store structured enterprise data, such as financial records, employee records, manufacturing, logistical information, and the like. By design, relational databases are structured with rigid schemas, or set of formulas that describe the structure of a database. Changes to those schemas can lead to broken functionality, introducing lengthy delays and risk when making changes. To build a search in a relational database, practitioners must usually make alterations to a schema.

Multidimensional databases are designed for analyzing large groups of records. The term OLAP (On-Line Analytical Processing) has become almost synonymous with "multidimensional database." OLAP tools enable users to analyze different dimensions of multidimensional data. Multidimensional databases are great for data mining and monthly reporting, but not for real-time events.

Machine data is at a much lower level of detail than transactional data. Transactional data might store all of the product, shipping, and payment data associated with an online purchase. The machine data associated with this purchase would include thousands of records, or events, that track every users' click, every page and image loaded, every ad requested, and so on. Machine data is not just about the finished result, or the destination, but about the entire journey!

Because it's so detailed, machine data can be used for a wide variety of purposes. In the world of IT, machine data can, for example, help find problems and also show whether systems are operating within typical ranges of performance. In the world of business, machine data can track consumer behavior and help segment consumers for targeted marketing messages.

To help you get a better idea of the nature of machine data, this appendix briefly describes some of the different types you may encounter.

Application Logs

Most homegrown and packaged applications write local log files, often by logging services built into middleware—WebLogic, WebSphere®, JBoss™, .NET™, PHP, and others. Log files are critical for day-to-day debugging of production applications by developers and application support. They're also often the best way to report on business and user activity and to detect fraud because they have all the details of transactions. When developers put timing information into their log events, log files can also be used to monitor and report on application performance.

Web Access Logs

Web access logs report every request processed by a web server—what client IP address it came from, what URL was requested, what the referring URL was, and data about the success or failure of the request. They're most commonly processed to produce web analytics reports for marketing—daily counts of visitors, most requested pages, and the like.

They're also invaluable as a starting point to investigate a user-reported problem because the log of a failed request can establish the exact time of an error. Web logs are fairly standard and well structured. The main challenge is in dealing with them is their sheer volume, as busy websites typically experience billions of hits a day as the norm.

Web Proxy Logs

Nearly all enterprises, service providers, institutions, and government organizations that provide employees, customers or guests with web access use some type of web proxy to control and monitor that access. Web proxies log every web request made by users through the proxy. They may include corporate usernames and URLs. These logs are critical for monitoring and investigating "terms of service" abuses or corporate web usage policy and are also a vital component of effective monitoring and investigation of data leakage.

Call Detail Records

Call Detail Records (CDRs), Charging Data Records, and Event Data Records are some of the names given to events logged by telecoms and network switches. CDRs contain useful details of a call or service that passed through the switch, such as the number making the call, the number receiving the call, call time, call duration, and type of call. As communications services move to Internet Protocol-based services, this data is also referred to as IPDRs, containing details such as IP address, port number, and the like. The specs, formats, and structure of these files vary enormously; keeping pace with all the permutations has traditionally been a challenge. Yet the data they contain is critical for billing, revenue assurance, customer assurance, partner settlements, marketing intelligence, and more. Splunk can quickly index the data and combine it with other business data to enable users to derive new insights from this rich usage information.

Clickstream Data

Use of a web page on a website is captured in clickstream data. This provides insight into what a user is doing and is useful for usability analysis, marketing, and general research. Formats for this data are nonstandard, and actions can be logged in multiple places, such as the web server, routers, proxy servers, and ad servers. Monitoring tools often look at a partial view of the data from a specific source. Web analytics and data warehouse products sample the data, thereby missing a complete view of behavior and offering no real-time analysis.

Message Queuing

Message queuing technologies such as TIBCO®, JMS, and AquaLogic™ are used to pass data and tasks between service and application components on a publish/subscribe basis. Subscribing to these message queues is a good way to debug problems in complex applications—you can see exactly what the next component down the chain received from the prior component. Separately, message queues are increasingly being used as the backbone of logging architectures for applications.

Packet Data

Data generated by networks is processed using tools such as tcpdump and tcpflow, which generate pcaps data and other useful packet-level and session-level information. This information is necessary to handle performance degradation, timeouts, bottlenecks, or suspicious activity that indicates that the network may be compromised or the object of a remote attack.

Configuration Files

There's no substitute for actual, active system configuration to understand how the infrastructure has been set up. Past configs are needed for debugging past failures that could recur. When configs change, it's important to know what changed and when, whether the change was authorized, and whether a successful attacker compromised the system to backdoors, time bombs, or other latent threats.

Database Audit Logs and Tables

Databases contain some of the most sensitive corporate data—customer records, financial data, patient records, and more. Audit records of all database queries are vital for understanding who accessed or changed what data when. Database audit logs are also useful for understanding how applications are using databases to optimize queries. Some databases log audit records to files, while others maintain audit tables accessible using SQL.

File System Audit Logs

The sensitive data that's not in databases is on file systems, often being shared. In some industries such as healthcare, the biggest data leakage risk is consumer records on shared file systems. Different operating systems, third party tools, and storage technologies provide different options for auditing read access to sensitive data at the file system level. This audit data is a vital data source for monitoring and investigating access to sensitive information.

Management and Logging APIs

Increasingly vendors are exposing critical management data and log events through standardized and proprietary APIs, rather than by them logging to files. Checkpoint® firewalls log using the OPSEC Log Export API (OPSEC LEA). Virtualization vendors, including VMware® and Citrix®, expose configurations, logs, and system status with their own APIs.

OS Metrics, Status, and Diagnostic Commands

Operating systems expose critical metrics, such as CPU and memory utilization and status information using command-line utilities like ps and iostat on Unix and Linux and perfmon on Windows. This data is usually harnessed by server monitoring tools but is rarely persisted, even though it's potentially invaluable for troubleshooting, analyzing trends to discover latent issues, and investigating security incidents.

Other Machine Data Sources

There are countless other useful and important machine data sources we did not describe, including source code repository logs, physical security logs, and so on. You still need firewall and IDS logs to report on network connections and attacks. OS logs, including Unix and Linux syslog and the Windows event logs, record who logged into your servers, what administrative actions they took, when services start and stop, and when kernel panics happen. Logs from DNS, DHCP, and other network services record who was assigned what IP address and how domains are resolved. Syslogs from your routers, switches, and network devices record the state of network connections and failures of critical network components. There's more to machine data than just logs and a much broader diversity of logs than traditional Log Management solutions can support.

Appendix B: Case Sensitivity

Some things in Splunk are case-sensitive, while others are not, as summarized in Table B-1.

Table B-1. Case sensitivity

	Sensitive	Insensitive	Examples
Command names		X	`TOP, top, sTaTs`
Command keywords		X	`AS used by stats, rename, ...;` `BY used by stats, chart, top, ...;` `WITH used by replace`
Search terms		X	`error, ERROR, Error`
Statistical functions		X	`avg, AVG, Avg used by stats, chart, ...`
Boolean operators	X (uppercase)		`AND, OR, NOT (boolean operators)` `vs. and, or, not (literal keywords)`
Field names	X		`host vs. HOST`
Field values		X	`host=localhost, host=LOCALhost`
Regular expressions	X		`\d\d\d vs. \D\D\D`
`replace` command	X		`error vs. ERROR`

Appendix C: Top Commands

Here are the most common search commands used by a sample of end-users and by Splunk apps.

Top Searches by End Users		Top Searches by Splunk Apps	
Command	Prevalence	Command	Prevalence
search	10964	search	1030
eval	4840	stats	232
fields	2045	timechart	215
stats	1840	eval	211
rename	1416	fields	142
timechart	1185	top	116
sort	1127	dedup	100
dedup	730	rename	96
fillnull	534	chart	79
rex	505	sort	76
table	487	rex	42
convert	467	head	29
metadata	451	multikv	26
loadjob	438	collect	25
chart	437	sitop	21
where	384	convert	20
append	373	where	17
join	314	fillnull	17
head	307	regex	17
top	280	format	16
transaction	260	lookup	14

makemv	209	outlier	12
rangemap	202	join	9
appendcols	201	replace	9
lookup	157	streamstats	8
replace	102		

Appendix D: Top Resources

We realize that this book can't tell you everything you need to know about Splunk. Here is a list of websites to continue your education. These links are also listed at http://splunk.com/goto/book#links.

Splunk download page	http://splunk.com/download
Splunk docs	http://docs.splunk.com
Splunk community	http://splunkbase.com
Community-based docs	http://innovato.com
Training videos	http://splunk.com/view/SP-CAAAGB6
Splunk videos	http://splunk.com/videos
Splunk blogs	http://blogs.splunk.com
Splunk TV	http://splunk.tv

Appendix E: Splunk Quick Reference Guide

CONCEPTS

Overview

Index-time Processing: Splunk reads data from a *source*, such as a file or port, on a *host* (e.g. "my machine"), classifies that *source* into a sourcetype (such as syslog, access_combined, or apache error), then extracts timestamps, breaks up the source into individual events (such as log events, alerts) which can consist of single or multiple lines, and writes each event into an *index* on disk, for later retrieval with a *search*.

Search-time Processing: When a *search* starts, matching indexed *events* are retrieved from disk, *fields* (such as code=404 or user=david,...) are extracted from the *event's* text, and the *event* is classified by matching against eventtype definitions (such as error or login). The *events* returned from a search can then be powerfully transformed using SPL to generate *reports* that display on *dashboards*.

Events

An *event* is one line of data. Here is an event in a web activity log:

```
173.26.34.223 - - [01/Jul/2009:12:05:27 -0700] "GET /trade/
app?action=logout HTTP/1.1" 200 2953
```

More specifically, an event is a set of values associated with a timestamp. While many events are short and only take up a line or two, others can be long, such as a whole text document, a config file, or whole Java stack trace. Splunk uses line-breaking rules to determine how it breaks these events up for display in the search results.

Sources and Sourcetypes

A source is the name of the file, stream, or other input from which an event originates—for example, /var/log/messages or UDP:514. *Sources* are classified into *sourcetypes*, which may be well-known, such as access_combined (web server logs) or can be created on the fly by Splunk when it sees a source with data and formatting it hasn't seen before. *Events* with the same *sourcetype* can come from different *sources*—events from the file /var/log/messages and from a syslog input on udp:514 can both have sourcetype=linux_syslog.

Hosts

A *host* is the name of the physical or virtual device from which an event originates. Hosts provide an easy way to find all data originating from a particular device.

Indexes

When you add data to Splunk, Splunk processes it, breaking the data into individual events, timestamps the events, and stores them in an *index* so that the data can be searched and analyzed later. By default, data you feed to Splunk is stored in the main *index*, but you can create and specify other indexes for Splunk to use for different data inputs.

Fields

Fields are searchable name/value pairings in *event* data. As Splunk processes *events* at index time and search time, it automatically extracts fields. At index time, Splunk extracts a small set of default fields for each *event*, including host, source, and sourcetype. At search time, Splunk extracts what can be a wide range of fields from the event data, including user-defined patterns and obvious field name/value pairs such as userid=jdoe.

Tags

Tags are aliases to *field* values. For example, if two host names refer to the same computer, you could give both host values the same tag (for example, hal9000). When you search for tag=hal9000, Splunk returns *events* involving both host name values.

Event Types

Event types are dynamic tags attached to an *event*, if it matches the search definition of the *event type*. For example, if you define an *event type* called `problem` with a search definition of `error OR warn OR fatal OR fail`, whenever a search result contains `error`, `warn`, `fatal`, or `fail`, the event has an `eventtype` field/value with `eventtype=problem`. If you were searching for `login`, the logins with problems would be annotated with `eventtype=problem`. *Event types* are cross-referenced searches that categorize *events* at search time.

Reports and Dashboards

Search results with formatting information (e.g., as a table or chart) are informally referred to as *reports*, and multiple *reports* can be placed on a common page, called a *dashboard*.

Apps

Apps are collections of Splunk configurations, objects, and code. *Apps* allow you to build different environments that sit on top of Splunk. You can have one app for troubleshooting email servers, one app for web analysis, and so on.

Permissions/Users/Roles

Saved Splunk objects, such as `savedsearches`, `eventtypes`, `reports`, and `tags`, enrich your data, making it easier to search and understand. These objects have *permissions* and can be kept private or shared with other users by roles (such as admin, power, or user). A *role* is a set of capabilities that you define, such as whether a particular role is allowed to add data or edit a report. Splunk with a free license does not support user authentication.

Transactions

A *transaction* is a set of events grouped into one for easier analysis. For example, because a customer shopping online generates multiple web access events with the same SessionID, it may be convenient to group those events into one transaction. With one transaction event, it's easier to generate statistics such as how long shoppers shopped, how many items they bought, which shoppers bought items and then returned them, and so on.

Forwarder/Indexer

A *forwarder* is a version of Splunk that allows you to send data to a central Splunk *indexer* or group of *indexers*. An *indexer* provides indexing capability for local and remote data.

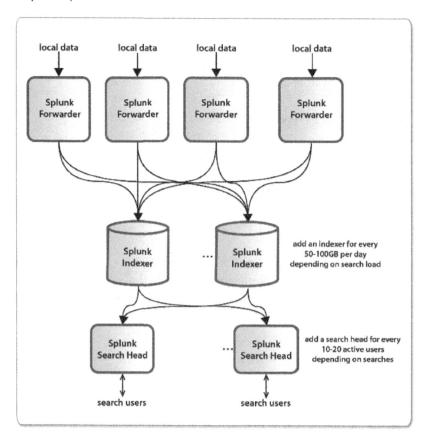

SPL

A *search* is a series of commands and arguments, chained together with pipe character (|) that takes the output of one command and feeds it into the next command.

```
search-args | cmd1 cmd-args | cmd2 cmd-args | ...
```

Search commands are used to take indexed data and filter unwanted information, extract more information, calculate values, transform them, and statistically analyze results. The search results retrieved from the index can be thought of as a dynamically created table. Each search command redefines the shape of that table. Each indexed event is a row, with columns for each field value. Columns include basic information about the data and data dynamically extracted at search-time.

At the head of each search is an implied search-the-index-for-events command, which can be used to search for keywords (e.g., `error`), boolean expressions (e.g., `(error OR failure) NOT success`), phrases (e.g., "database error"), wildcards (e.g., `fail*` matches fail, fails, and failure), field values (e.g., `code=404`), inequality (e.g., `code!=404` or `code>200`), a field having any value or no value (e.g., `code=*` or `NOT code=*`). For example, the search:

```
sourcetype="access_combined" error | top 10 uri
```

retrieves indexed `access_combined` events from disk that contain the term `error` (ANDs are implied between search terms), and then for those events, reports the top 10 most common URI values.

Subsearches

A *subsearch* is an argument to a command that runs its own search, returning those results to the parent command as the argument value. *Subsearches* are enclosed in square brackets. For example, this command finds all syslog events from the user with the last login error:

```
sourcetype=syslog [search login error | return user]
```

Note that the *subsearch* returns one user value because by default the `return` command returns one value, although there are options to return more (e.g., `| return 5 user`).

Relative Time Modifiers

Besides using the custom-time ranges in the user interface, you can specify in your search the time ranges of retrieved events with the `latest` and `earliest` search modifiers. The relative times are specified with a string of characters that indicate amount of time (integer and unit) and, optionally, a "snap to" time unit:

```
[+|-]<time_integer><time_unit>@<snap_time_unit>
```

For example, `error earliest=-1d@d latest=-1h@h` retrieves events containing `error` that from yesterday (snapped to midnight) to the last hour (snapped to the hour).

Time Units: Specified as second (`s`), minute (`m`), hour (`h`), day (`d`), week (`w`), month (`mon`), quarter(`q`), or year (`y`). The preceding value defaults to 1 (i.e., `m` is the same as `1m`).

Snapping: Indicates the nearest or latest time to which your time amount rounds down. Snapping rounds down to the most recent time that is not after the specified time. For example, if it's 11:59:00 and you "snap to" hours (@h), you snap to 11:00, not 12:00. You can snap to a day of the week, too; use @w0 for Sunday, @w1 for Monday, and so on.

COMMON SEARCH COMMANDS

COMMAND	
chart/timechart	Returns results in a tabular output for (time series) charting.
dedup	Removes subsequent results that match.
eval	Calculates an expression. (See EVAL FUNCTIONS table.)
fields	Removes fields from search results.
head/tail	Returns the first/last N results.
lookup	Adds field values from an external source.
rename	Renames a specified field; wildcards can be used to specify multiple fields.
replace	Replaces values of specified fields with a specified new value.
rex	Specifies regular expression to use to extract fields.
search	Filters results to those that match the search expression.
sort	Sorts search results by the specified fields.
stats	Provides statistics, grouped optionally by fields.
top/rare	Displays the most/least common values of a field.
transaction	Groups search results into transactions.

Optimizing Searches

The key to fast searching is to limit the data to read from disk to an absolute minimum and then to filter that data as early as possible in the search so that processing is done on the smallest amount of data.

Partition data into separate indexes if you'll rarely perform searches across multiple types of data. For example, put web data in one index and firewall data in another.

More tips:

- Search as specifically as you can (`fatal_error`, not `*error*`).
- Limit the time range (e.g., `-1h` not `-1w`).
- Filter out unneeded fields as soon as possible.
- Filter out results as soon as possible before calculations.
- For report generating searches, use the **Advanced Charting** view, and not the **Timeline** view, which calculates timelines.
- Turn off the **Field Discovery** switch when not needed.
- Use summary indexes to precalculate commonly used values.
- Make sure your disk I/O is the fastest you have available.

SEARCH EXAMPLES

Filter Results	
Filter results to only include those with `fail` in their raw text and `status=0`.	`... | search fail status=0`
Remove duplicates of results with the same host value.	`... | dedup host`
Keep only search results whose _raw field contains IP addresses in the nonroutable class A (10.0.0.0/8).	`... | regex _raw="(?<!\d)10.\ d{1,3}\.\d{1,3}\.\d{1,3} (?!\d)"`
Group Results	
Cluster results together, sort by their `cluster_count` values, and then return the 20 largest clusters (in data size).	`... | cluster t=0.9 showcount=true | sort limit=20 -cluster_count`
Group results that have the same host and cookie, occur within 30 seconds of each other, and do not have a pause greater than 5 seconds between each event into a transaction.	`... | transaction host cookie maxspan=30s maxpause=5s`
Group results with the same IP address (`clientip`) and where the first result contains signon and the last result contains purchase.	`... | transaction clientip startswith="signon" endswith="purchase"`

Order Results	
Return the first 20 results.	`...	head 20`
Reverse the order of a result set.	`...	reverse`
Sort results by `ip` value (in ascending order) and then by `url` value (in descending order).	`...	sort ip, -url`
Return the last 20 results (in reverse order).	`...	tail 20`

Reporting	
Return events with uncommon values.	`...	anomalousvalue action=filter pthresh=0.02`
Return the maximum "delay" by "size", where "size" is broken down into a maximum of 10 equal sized buckets.	`...	chart max(delay) by size bins=10`
Return max(delay) for each value of foo split by the value of bar.	`...	chart max(delay) over foo by bar`
Return max(delay) for each value of foo.	`...	chart max(delay) over foo`
Remove all outlying numerical values.	`...	outlier`
Remove duplicates of results with the same host value and return the total count of the remaining results.	`...	stats dc(host)`
Return the average for each hour of any unique field that ends with the string lay (such as delay, xdelay, and relay).	`...	stats avg(*lay) by date_hour`
Calculate the average value of CPU each minute for each host.	`...	timechart span=1m avg(CPU) by host`
Create a timechart of the count of from web sources by host.	`...	timechart count by host`
Return the 20 most common values of the `url` field.	`...	top limit=20 url`
Return the least common values of the `url` field.	`...	rare url`

Add Fields	
Set velocity to distance / time.	`... | eval velocity=distance/time`
Extract from and to fields using regular expressions. If a raw event contains `From: Susan To: David`, then `from=Susan` and `to=David`.	`... | rex field=_raw "From: (?<from>.*) To: (?<to>.*)"`
Save the running total of count in a field called `total_count`.	`... | accum count as total_count`
For each event where `count` exists, compute the difference between `count` and its previous value and store the result in `countdiff`.	`... | delta count as countdiff`

Filter Fields	
Keep the `host` and `ip` fields, and display them in the order: `host, ip`.	`... | fields + host, ip`
Remove the `host` and `ip` fields.	`... | fields - host, ip`

Modify Fields	
Keep the host and ip fields, and display them in the order: host, ip.	`... | fields + host, ip`
Remove the host and ip fields.	`... | fields - host, ip`

Multivalued Fields	
Combine the multiple values of the `recipients` field into one value.	`... | nomv recipients`
Separate the values of the `recipients` field into multiple field values, displaying the top recipients.	`... | makemv delim="," recipients | top recipients`
Create new results for each value of the multivalue field `recipients`.	`... | mvexpand recipients`
Combine each result that is identical except for its `RecordNumber`, setting `RecordNumber` to a multivalued field with all the varying values.	`... | fields EventCode, Category, RecordNumber | mvcombine delim="," RecordNumber`
Find the number of `recipient` values.	`... | eval to_count = mvcount(recipients)`
Find the first email address in the `recipient` field.	`... | eval recipient_first = mvindex(recipient,0)`

Find all recipient values that end in .net or .org	`... | eval netorg_recipients = mvfilter(match(recipient, "\.net$") OR match(recipient, "\.org$"))`
Find the combination of the values of foo, "bar", and the values of baz.	`... | eval newval = mvappend(foo, "bar", baz)`
Find the index of the first recipient value that matches "\.org$"	`... | eval orgindex = mvfind(recipient, "\.org$")`
Lookup Tables	
Look up the value of each event's user field in the lookup table usertogroup, setting the event's group field.	`... | lookup usertogroup user output group`
Write the search results to the lookup file users.csv.	`... | outputlookup users.csv`
Read in the lookup file users.csv as search results.	`... | inputlookup users.csv`

EVAL FUNCTIONS

The eval command calculates an expression and puts the resulting value into a field (e.g., "...| eval force = mass * acceleration"). The following table lists the functions eval understands, in addition to basic arithmetic operators (+ - * / %), string concatenation (e.g., '...| eval name = last . ", " . last'), and Boolean operations (AND OR NOT XOR < > <= >= != = == LIKE).

Eval Functions Table

Function	Description	Examples
abs(X)	Returns the absolute value of X.	abs(number)
case(X,"Y",…)	Takes pairs of arguments X and Y, where X arguments are Boolean expressions that, when evaluated to TRUE, return the corresponding Y argument.	case(error == 404, "Not found", error == 500,"Internal Server Error", error == 200, "OK")
ceil(X)	Ceiling of a number X.	ceil(1.9)
cidrmatch("X",Y)	Identifies IP addresses that belong to a subnet.	cidrmatch("123.132.32.0/25",ip)

`coalesce(X,…)`	Returns the first value that is not null.	`coalesce(null(), "Returned val", null())`
`exact(X)`	Evaluates an expression X using double precision floating point arithmetic.	`exact(3.14*num)`
`exp(X)`	Returns eX.	`exp(3)`
`floor(X)`	Returns the floor of a number X.	`floor(1.9)`
`if(X,Y,Z)`	If X evaluates to TRUE, the result is the second argument Y. If X evaluates to FALSE, the result evaluates to the third argument Z.	`if(error==200, "OK", "Error")`
`isbool(X)`	Returns TRUE if X is Boolean.	`isbool(field)`
`isint(X)`	Returns TRUE if X is an integer.	`isint(field)`
`isnotnull(X)`	Returns TRUE if X is not NULL.	`isnotnull(field)`
`isnull(X)`	Returns TRUE if X is NULL.	`isnull(field)`
`isnum(X)`	Returns TRUE if X is a number.	`isnum(field)`
`isstr()`	Returns TRUE if X is a string.	`isstr(field)`
`len(X)`	This function returns the character length of a string X.	`len(field)`
`like(X,"Y")`	Returns TRUE if and only if X is like the SQLite pattern in Y.	`like(field, "foo%")`
`ln(X)`	Returns the natural log of X.	`ln(bytes)`
`log(X,Y)`	Returns the log of the first argument X using the second argument Y as the base. Y defaults to 10.	`log(number,2)`

`lower(X)`	Returns the lowercase of X.	`lower(username)`
`ltrim(X,Y)`	Returns X with the characters in Y trimmed from the left side. Y defaults to spaces and tabs.	`ltrim(" ZZZabcZZ ", " Z")`
`match(X,Y)`	Returns True, if X matches the regex pattern Y.	`match(field, "^\d{1,3}\.\d$")`
`max(X,…)`	Returns the greater of the two values.	`max(delay, mydelay)`
`md5(X)`	Returns the MD5 hash of string value X.	`md5(field)`
`min(X,…)`	Returns the min.	`min(delay, mydelay)`
`mvcount(X)`	Returns the number of values of X.	`mvcount(multifield)`
`mvfilter(X)`	Filters a multivalued field based on the Boolean expression X.	`mvfilter(match(email, "net$"))`
`mvindex(X,Y,Z)`	Returns a subset of the multivalued field X from start position (zero-based) Y to Z (optional).	`mvindex( multi-field, 2)`
`mvjoin(X,Y)`	Given a multivalued field X and string delimiter Y, joins the individual values of X using Y.	`mvjoin(foo, ";")`
`now()`	Returns the current time, represented in Unix time.	`now()`
`null()`	Takes no arguments and returns NULL.	`null()`
`nullif(X,Y)`	Given two arguments, fields X and Y, returns X if the arguments are different; returns NULL, otherwise.	`nullif(fieldA, fieldB)`
`pi()`	Returns the constant pi.	`pi()`
`pow(X,Y)`	Returns XY.	`pow(2,10)`

`random()`	Returns a pseudo-random number ranging from 0 to 2147483647.	`random()`
`relative_time(X,Y)`	Given epochtime time X and relative time specifier Y, returns the epochtime value of Y applied to X.	`relative_ time(now(),"-1d@d")`
`replace(X,Y,Z)`	Returns a string formed by substituting string Z for every occurrence of regex string Y in string X.	`Returns date with the month and day numbers switched, so if the in- put is 1/12/2009 the return value is 12/1/2009: replace(date, "^(\d{1,2})/ (\d{1,2})/", "\2/\1/")`
`round(X,Y)`	Returns X rounded to the amount of decimal places specified by Y. The default is to round to an integer.	`round(3.5)`
`rtrim(X,Y)`	Returns X with the characters in Y trimmed from the right side. If Y is not specified, spaces and tabs are trimmed.	`rtrim(" ZZZZabcZZ ", " Z")`
`searchmatch(X)`	Returns true if the event matches the search string X.	`searchmatch("foo AND bar")`
`split(X,"Y")`	Returns X as a multivalued field, split by delimiter Y.	`split(foo, ";")`
`sqrt(X)`	Returns the square root of X.	`sqrt(9)`
`strftime(X,Y)`	Returns epochtime value X rendered using the format specified by Y.	`strftime(_time, "%H:%M")`

`strptime(X,Y)`	Given a time represented by a string X, returns value parsed from format Y.	`strptime(timeStr, "%H:%M")`
`substr(X,Y,Z)`	Returns a substring field X from start position (1-based) Y for Z (optional) characters.	`substr("string", 1, 3) +substr("string", -3)`
`time()`	Returns the wall-clock time with microsecond resolution.	`time()`
`tonumber(X,Y)`	Converts input string X to a number, where Y (optional, defaults to 10) defines the base of the number to convert to.	`tonumber("0A4",16)`
`tostring(X,Y)`	Returns a field value of X as a string. If X is a number, it reformats it as a string; if a Boolean value, either "True" or "False". If X is a number, the second argument Y is optional and can either be "hex" (convert X to hexadecimal), "commas" (formats X with commas and 2 decimal places), or "duration" (converts seconds X to readable time format HH:MM:SS).	This example returns foo=615 and foo2=00:10:15: `... | eval foo=615 |eval foo2=tostring(foo," duration")`
`trim(X,Y)`	Returns X with the characters in Y trimmed from both sides. If Y is not specified, spaces and tabs are trimmed.	`trim(" ZZZZabcZZ ", " Z")`
`typeof(X)`	Returns a string representation of its type.	This example returns: "NumberStringBoolInvalid": `typeof(12)+ typeof("string")+ typeof(1==2)+ typeof(badfield)`

upper(X)	Returns the uppercase of X.	upper(username)
urldecode(X)	Returns the URL X decoded.	urldecode("http%3A%2F%2Fwww.splunk.com%2Fdownload%3Fr%3Dheader")
validate(X,Y,...)	Given pairs of arguments, Boolean expressions X and strings Y, returns the string Y corresponding to the first expression X that evaluates to False and defaults to NULL if all are True.	validate(isint(port), "ERROR: Port is not an integer", port >= 1 AND port <= 65535, "ERROR: Port is out of range")

COMMON STATS FUNCTIONS

Common statistical functions used with the chart, stats, and timechart commands. Field names can be wildcarded, so avg(*delay) might calculate the average of the delay and xdelay fields.

Function	Description
avg(X)	Returns the average of the values of field X.
count(X)	Returns the number of occurrences of the field X. To indicate a field value to match, format X as eval(field="value").
dc(X)	Returns the count of distinct values of the field X.
first(X)	Returns the first seen value of the field X. In general, the first seen value of the field is the chronologically most recent instance of field.
last(X)	Returns the last seen value of the field X.
list(X)	Returns the list of all values of the field X as a multivalue entry. The order of the values reflects the order of input events.
max(X)	Returns the maximum value of the field X. If the values of X are non-numeric, the max is found from lexicographic ordering.
median(X)	Returns the middle-most value of the field X.
min(X)	Returns the minimum value of the field X. If the values of X are non-numeric, the min is found from lexicographic ordering.
mode(X)	Returns the most frequent value of the field X.

perc<X>(Y)	Returns the X-th percentile value of the field Y. For example, perc5(total) returns the 5th percentile value of a field total..
range(X)	Returns the difference between the max and min values of the field X.
stdev(X)	Returns the sample standard deviation of the field X.
stdevp(X)	Returns the population standard deviation of the field X.
sum(X)	Returns the sum of the values of the field X.
sumsq(X)	Returns the sum of the squares of the values of the field X.
values(X)	Returns the list of all distinct values of the field X as a multivalue entry. The order of the values is lexicographical.
var(X)	Returns the sample variance of the field X.

REGULAR EXPRESSIONS

Regular expressions are useful in many areas, including search commands `regex` and `rex`; `eval` functions `match()` and `replace()`; and in field extraction.

REGEX	NOTE	EXAMPLE	EXPLANATION
\s	white space	\d\s\d	digit space digit
\S	not white space	\d\S\d	digit non-whitespace digit
\d	Digit	\d\d\d-\d\d-\d\d\d\d	SSN
\D	not digit	\D\D\D	three non-digits
\w	word character (letter, number, or _)	\w\w\w	three word chars
\W	not a word character	\W\W\W	three non-word chars
[...]	any included character	[a-z0-9#]	any char that is a thru z, 0 thru 9, or #
[^...]	no included character	[^xyx]	any char but x, y, or z
*	zero or more	\w*	zero or more words chars
+	one or more	\d+	integer

?	zero of one	\d\d\d-?\d\d-?\d\d\d\d	SSN with dashes being optional
|	Or	\w|\d	word or digit character
(?P<var> ...)	named extraction	(?P<ssn>\d\d\d-\d\d\-\d\d\d\d)	pull out a SSN and assign to 'ssn' field
(?: ...)	logical grouping	(?:\w|\d) | (?:\d|\w)	word-char then digit OR digit then word-char
^	start of line	^\d+	line begins with at least one digit
$	end of line	\d+$	line ends with at least one digit
{...}	number of repetitions	\d{3,5}	between 3-5 digits
\	Escape	\[	escape the [char
(?= ...)	Lookahead	(?=\D)error	error must be preceded by a non-digit
(?! ...)	negative lookahead	(?!\d)error	error cannot be preceded by a digit

COMMON SPLUNK STRPTIME FUNCTIONS

strptime formats are useful for eval functions strftime() and strptime() and for timestamping event data.

TIME	%H	24 hour (leading zeros) (00 to 23)
	%I	12 hour (leading zeros) (01 to 12)
	%M	Minute (00 to 59)
	%S	Second (00 to 61)
	%N	subseconds with width (%3N = millisecs, %6N = microsecs, %9N = nanosecs)
	%p	AM or PM
	%Z	Time zone (GMT)
	%s	Seconds since 1/1/1970 (1308677092)

DAYS	%d	Day of month (leading zeros) (01 to 31)
	%j	Day of year (001 to 366)
	%w	Weekday (0 to 6)
	%a	Abbreviated weekday (Sun)
	%A	Weekday (Sunday)
	%b	Abbreviated month name (Jan)
	%B	Month name (January)
	%m	Month number (01 to 12)
	%y	Year without century (00 to 99)
	%Y	Year (2008)
	%Y-%m-%d	1998-12-31
	%y-%m-%d	98-12-31
	%b %d, %Y	Jan 24, 2003
	%B %d, %Y	January 24, 2003
	q|%d %b '%y = %Y-%m-%d	q|25 Feb '03 = 2003-02-25|

CPSIA information can be obtained at www.ICGtesting.com
Printed in the USA
LVOW03s2008250315

431962LV00005B/54/P